Make Your Own Simple Will

(+CD-ROM)

Fourth Edition

Mark Warda

Attorney at Law

SPHINX® PUBLISHING

AN IMPRINT OF SOURCEBOOKS, INC.®
NAPERVILLE, ILLINOIS
www.SphinxLegal.com

Fourth Edition: 2006

Published by: **Sphinx® Publishing, An Imprint of Sourcebooks, Inc.®**

Naperville Office
P.O. Box 4410
Naperville, Illinois 60567-4410
630-961-3900
Fax: 630-961-2168
www.sourcebooks.com
www.SphinxLegal.com

This publication is designed to provide accurate and authoritative information in regard to the subject matter covered. It is sold with the understanding that the publisher is not engaged in rendering legal, accounting, or other professional service. If legal advice or other expert assistance is required, the services of a competent professional person should be sought.

From a Declaration of Principles Jointly Adopted by a Committee of the American Bar Association and a Committee of Publishers and Associations

This product is not a substitute for legal advice.

Disclaimer required by Texas statutes.

Library of Congress Cataloging-in-Publication Data
Warda, Mark.
  Make your own simple will (+CD-ROM) / by Mark Warda.-- 4th ed.
     p. cm.
  Rev. ed.: How to make your own simple will. 3rd ed. 2002.
  Includes bibliographical references and index.
  ISBN-10 1-57248-511-6
  ISBN-13: 978-1-57248-511-2 (pbk. : alk. paper)
  1. Wills--United States--Popular works. 2. Estate planning--United States--Popular works. I. Warda, Mark. How to make your own simple will. II. Title.

KF755.Z9W35 2006
346.7305'4--dc22
                                                    2005014838

Printed and bound in the United States of America.
BG — 10 9 8 7 6 5 4 3 2 1

without that person's signature. If you put your bank account in joint ownership with someone, he or she can take out all of your money.

Example 1:

Alice put her house in joint ownership with her son. She later married Ed and moved in with him. She wanted to sell her house and invest the money for income. Her son refused to sign the deed because he wanted to keep the home in the family. She was in court for ten months getting her house back and the judge almost refused to do it.

Example 2:

Alex put his bank accounts into joint ownership with his daughter, Mary, to avoid probate. Mary fell in love with Doug, who was in trouble with the law. Doug talked Mary into *borrowing* $30,000 from the account for a *business deal* that went sour. Later she *borrowed* $25,000 more to pay Doug's bail bond. Alex did not find out until it was too late that his money was gone.

TENANCY IN COMMON

Property that is not owned in joint tenancy with right of survivorship or in tenancy by the entireties is owned in a *tenancy in common*. This means that each person owns part of the property (such as one-half or one-third), and upon each person's death, the property goes to his or her heirs or beneficiaries, not to the other owner.

Example:

Tom and Marcia bought a house together and lived together for twenty years, but were never married. The deed did not specify joint tenancy. When Tom died, his brother inherited his half of the house, and it had to be sold because Marcia could not afford to buy it from him.

A SPOUSE OVERRULING A WILL

Under the laws of most states, a surviving spouse is entitled to a percentage of a person's estate no matter what the person's will states. This percentage can range from one-quarter to one-half, and is usually called an *elective share* or a *forced share*. The share is only calculated on the assets passing through probate in some states, but in others, the share includes property that avoids probate. In some states, the share depends on whether the property is *marital property* or *separate property*. This is determined by whether the property was acquired before or during the marriage, mixed with marital property, or came from some source outside the marriage. In some states, a spouse can claim a portion of the estate only for the term of his or her life.

Example 1:

John owns a $1,000,000 ranch with his brother in joint tenancy with right of survivorship and $1,000,000 in stock in his own name. His will leaves his stock to his children by a prior marriage, but nothing to his wife because she is wealthier than him and does not need the money. Unless John has a premarital or marital agreement, his wife would be entitled to claim one-third of the stock (in some states). In other states, his wife could claim one-half of the stock and one-half of the ranch.

Example 2:

Mary puts half of her property in a joint account with her husband and in her will she leaves all of her other property to her sister. When she dies, her husband gets all the money in the joint account and 30% of all her other property.

If you do not plan to leave your spouse at least the amount of property your state allows by statute, you should consult a lawyer. Appendix A contains a state-by-state list of the spouse's share as of the time of completion of this manuscript. (Laws are amended regularly, so you should check your state law for changes.)

AVOIDING A SPOUSE'S SHARE

While some feel it is wrong to avoid giving a spouse the share allowed by law, there are legitimate reasons for doing so (such as where there are children from a prior marriage) and the law allows exceptions.

The safest way is for both spouses to sign a written agreement, either before or after the marriage, waiving any share the law may give them in each other's estates. In some states, a spouse's share can be avoided partially or completely by owning property in joint tenancy or in a trust. It is necessary in some cases, but not in all, to have the spouse sign over any interest he or she may have.

Example:

Dan owns his stocks jointly with his son. He owns his bank accounts jointly with his daughter. If he has no other property, in many states his spouse gets nothing since there is no property in his estate.

This is what would happen in a state where the spouse is entitled to a share of the *probate estate*. However, in some states, the spouse would be entitled to a share of the *augmented estate*. These are all assets that passed upon the death of the owner (such as joint property, life insurance, and beneficial interests in trusts). See Appendix A for your state's laws. Keep in mind that these laws can change at any time, so if this is a concern to you, check with an estate planning attorney.

Another way to provide for someone other than your spouse is with a life insurance policy naming that someone explicitly as the beneficiary. However, in some states, this can also be included in the estate.

Avoiding a spouse's share, especially without his or her knowledge, opens the possibility of a lawsuit after your death. If your actions were not done to precise legal requirements, the will could be overruled by a court. Therefore, you should consider consulting an attorney if you plan to leave your spouse less than the share provided by law.

I/T/F BANK ACCOUNTS VERSUS JOINT OWNERSHIP

One way of keeping bank accounts out of your estate and still retaining control is to title them *in trust for,* or I/T/F, with a named beneficiary. Some banks may use the letters POD for *pay on death* or TOD for *transfer on death*. Either way, the result is the same. No one except you can get the money until your death, and on death it immediately goes directly to the person you name, without a will or probate proceeding. These are sometimes called *Totten Trusts*, after the court case that declared them legal.

Example:

Rich opened a bank account in the name of "Rich, I/T/F Mary." If Rich dies, the money automatically goes to Mary. Prior to his death, Mary has no control over the account—she does not even have to know about it—and Rich can take Mary's name off the account at any time.

SECURITIES REGISTERED AS I/T/F

Initially, the drawback of the Totten Trust was that it was only good for cash in a bank account. Stocks and bonds still had to go through probate. Beginning in 1990, states began enacting a new law allowing I/T/F accounts for securities. These can include stocks, bonds, mutual funds, and other similar investments. Now an estate with cash and securities can pass on death with no need for court proceedings.

At the time of publication of this book, the law has been passed by forty-six states. Check with your mutual fund, stock broker, or attorney, or in your state statutes. The law is called the Uniform TOD Securities Registration Act. The states that have passed this law are listed in Appendix A.

To set up your securities to transfer automatically on death, you need to have them correctly registered. If you use a brokerage account, the brokerage company should have a form for you to do this.

If your state has not passed this law, you may be able to benefit from it by moving your securities account to a firm in a state that has passed this law. Check with different stock brokers and mutual fund companies to see if they allow you to set up your account to transfer on death.

If your securities are registered in your own name or with your spouse, you need to reregister them in TOD format with the designation of your beneficiary. The following are examples of how it is done in many states. Check with your mutual fund or stock broker for the proper way in your state or get a copy of the statute cited in the appendix.

Example 1:
Sole owner with sole beneficiary:

John S. Brown TOD John S. Brown Jr.

Example 2:
Multiple owners with sole beneficiary: John and Mary are joint tenants with right of survivorship, and when they die, John Jr. inherits the property.

John S. Brown Mary B. Brown JT TEN TOD
John S. Brown Jr.

Example 3:
Multiple owners—substituted beneficiary: John and Mary are joint tenants with right of survivorship, and when they die, John Jr. inherits the property. If John predeceases them, then Peter inherits it.

John S. Brown Mary B. Brown JT TEN TOD
John S. Brown Jr. SUB BEN Peter Q. Brown

Example 4:
Multiple owners—lineal descendants: John and Mary are joint tenants with right of survivorship, and when they die John Jr. inherits the property. If John predeceases them in death, then John Jr.'s lineal descendants inherit it.

John S. Brown Mary B. Brown JT TEN TOD
John S. Brown Jr. LDPS

RULES FOR HOMESTEADS

In some states, there are special rules for who can inherit your homestead. If you have a spouse, minor children, or both, you may not be able to leave the home to anyone but them. Homestead laws in some states cannot be claimed by creditors of the estate. If you have a spouse or minor children, and plan to leave your homestead to anyone but them, you should see a lawyer.

PROPERTY EXEMPT FROM YOUR WILL

If you have a spouse or minor children, then a certain amount of household furniture, furnishings, appliances, and automobiles in your name that are regularly used by you or members of your family are exempt from your will. This is called *exempt property*. If you have a spouse, your spouse gets this property. If you have no spouse, your children get it. Additionally, a spouse or minor children may get a *family allowance*.

Example:
Donna dies with a will giving half her property to her husband and half to her grown son from a previous marriage. Donna's property consists of a $5,000 automobile, $5,000 in furniture, and $10,000 in cash. Donna's husband may be able to get the car and the furniture as exempt property, and $6,000 as a family allowance. Then he and the son would split

the remaining $4,000. (The son would get even less if the husband also claimed a spouse's share as described on page 7.)

In some states, one can avoid having property declared exempt by specifically giving it to someone in a will. If items are given to certain persons, those items will not be considered part of the exempt property. Cash kept in a joint or I/T/F bank account would go to the joint owner or beneficiary, and would not be used as the family allowance. If this may be an issue in your estate, you should check with a lawyer.

MARRIAGE AND CHANGING YOUR WILL

In some states, if you get married after making your will and do not rewrite it after the wedding, your spouse gets a share of your estate as if you had no will, unless you have a premarital agreement, made a provision for your spouse in the will, or stated specifically in the will that you intended not to mention your prospective spouse.

Example:
John made his will leaving everything to his brother. When John married Joan, an heiress with plenty of money, he did not change his will because he still wanted his brother to get his estate. When he died, Joan got his entire estate and his brother got nothing.

The two issues involved are whether the spouse can get a share in spite of the will and if the marriage completely voids the will. If you get married and wish to leave your property to someone other than your spouse, you should consult an attorney.

DIVORCE AND YOUR WILL

In some states, getting divorced automatically deletes your former spouse's share from your will. You should not rely on this and should make a new will. If your spouse tries to get a share of the estate because he or she is mentioned, it may cost your estate considerable legal fees to defeat the claim.

Example:

George and Eunice made their wills leaving half their property to each other and half to their children from their previous marriages. After their divorce, George forgot to make a new will. When George died, Eunice hired a lawyer to file papers claiming half the estate. His children's lawyer pointed out that her share was void because of the divorce, but the other lawyer demanded a trial, hoping the children would settle the case by giving his client a few thousand dollars. They refused to settle and their attorney charged $5,000 for the trial.

In some states, divorce does *not* revoke your will. If you do not have time to make a new will after your divorce, you may want to revoke your will. This can be done by tearing it up or through other means discussed in Chapter 5. By revoking your will, you are choosing to use your state's distribution system of deciding your heirs, which, in all cases, would not include your ex-spouse. (see Chapter 2.)

CHILDREN AND YOUR WILL

In most states, having a child would change your will so that the new child would get a share equal to that of any other children. However, in some states, having a child may revoke your will or result in the new child getting a larger share than the other children.

Example:

Dave made a will leaving half his estate to his sister and the other half to his three children. He later had another child and did not revise his will. In some states, upon his death, his fourth child would get one quarter of his estate, his sister would get three-eighths, and the other three children would each get one-eighth.

It is best to rewrite your will at the birth of a child. However, another solution is to include the following clause after the names of your children in your will.

> "...and any afterborn children living at the time of my death, in equal shares."

HEIRS OR PARENTS HAVE A FORCED SHARE IN PUERTO RICO

Under the laws of Puerto Rico, your heirs have a legal right to a portion of your estate. Besides the right of your spouse to one-half of the marital property, your children (if any) have a legal right to two-thirds of your estate. Half of this amount is divided equally and the other half can be divided as you desire.

If you do not have any children (in or out of wedlock), then your parents, if living, are entitled to one-half of your estate.

YOUR DEBTS

One of the duties of the person administering an estate is to pay the debts of the decedent. Before an estate is distributed, the legitimate debts must be ascertained and paid.

An exception is *secured debts*. These are debts that are protected by a lien against property, like a home loan or a car loan. In the case of a secured debt, the loan does not have to be paid before the property is distributed.

Example:

John owns a $300,000 house with a $250,000 mortgage and he has $300,000 in the bank. If he leaves the house to his brother and the bank account to his sister, his brother would get the home but would owe the $250,000 mortgage.

What if your debts are more than your property? Today, unlike hundreds of years ago, people cannot inherit other peoples' debts. A person's property is used to pay their probate and funeral expenses first, and if there is not enough left to pay their other debts, then the creditors are out of luck. However, if a person leaves property to people and does not have enough assets to pay his or her debts, the property will be sold to pay the debts.

Example:

Jeb's will leaves all of his property to his three children. At the time of his death, Jeb, has $30,000 in medical bills and $11,000 in credit card debt, and his only assets are his car and $5,000 in stock. The car and stock would be sold, and the funeral bill and probate fees paid out of the proceeds. If any money was left, it would go to the creditors, and nothing would be left for the children. However, the children would not have to pay the balances on the medical bills or credit card debt.

In many states, the creditors of a deceased person can only make claims against property that goes through probate. This means that if a person sets up his or her property so that it all avoids probate, any debts remaining at his or her death will not have to be paid.

Example:

When Chris died, he owned a $200,000 house with his wife, a $25,000 bank account with his wife, a ranch worth $500,000 owned jointly with his brother, and $20,000 in stock in trust for his children. His debts were $5,000 on a personal credit card and a $20,000 line of credit in his name alone. Because all of his property will pass to people without a probate, in many states, his debts will not have to be paid, and the heirs will get the property free and clear.

ESTATE AND INHERITANCE TAXES

Estate taxes are levied against the amount in the estate. *Inheritance taxes* are levied against what is received by a person as an inheritance from an estate.

The federal government presently only taxes estates of $2,000,000 and higher. This amount will rise to $3,500,000 by 2009. In 2010 the tax is scheduled for complete repeal, then in 2011 it comes back with the exemption back down to $1,000,000. Most likely, the law will change again before 2011, so you would be well advised to keep up with changes. The following chart shows how the exempt estates are scheduled to rise.

Year	Exempt Amount
2006–2008	$2,000,000
2009	$3,500,000
2010	Unlimited
2011	$1,000,000

The amounts in the above table are called the *unified credit*. This is the amount of the estate exempt from tax. The unified credit applies to the estate a person leaves at death as well as to gifts during the lifetime. This means that if you make a gift of, say, $50,000 during your life, then the unified credit on your estate will be $50,000 lower than the above amounts.

Example:

Just before his death in 2006, Phillip gave $500,000 to his sister. When his estate was probated, the first $2,000,000 of his $3,000,000 estate was exempt from tax and the rest was subject to federal estate taxes.

However, there is also an *annual exclusion* of $11,000 per person. This means that every year you can give any person $11,000 and it will not count toward the unified credit. A married couple can receive double this amount, or $22,000. The amount will be indexed for inflation, but only in $1,000 increments once the total inflation reaches that amount.

Example:
Edna would like to give her five children each $50,000. She gives them each $10,000 per year for five years so it does not take away from her unified credit.

State Taxes

There is a big difference among the states as to whether and how most estates are taxed. Most states do not tax estates, unless the estates are very large, and then they only take as tax an amount that would have gone to the federal government anyway.

The following states have estate or inheritance taxes, and they range as high as 32%. All of these exempt the spouse, except Maryland and Mississippi. Some of them exempt smaller estates or children. If you have a large estate and live in one of these states, you should check with a tax advisor to see how much tax your estate or beneficiaries will have to pay.

Connecticut	Maryland	Oregon
Indiana	Massachusetts	Pennsylvania
Iowa	Nebraska	Puerto Rico
Kansas	New Jersey	Rhode Island
Kentucky	New York	Tennessee
Louisiana	Ohio	Washington
Maine	Oklahoma	Wisconsin

Because the federal estate tax is changing, states are amending their taxes. Check with your state department of revenue for any recent changes.

By setting up a primary residence in another state, you may be able to avoid estate taxes. Remember that most states have income or capital gains taxes. States that have no income, capital gains, estate, or inheritance taxes are Alaska, Florida, Nevada, Texas, and Wyoming.

The following website has information on the taxes of each state:

www.retirementliving.com

SOCIAL SECURITY

Entitlement to Social Security benefits ends at death. The payments are made in arrears. For example, the May 1st payment is for the month of April, so if a person dies May 2nd, you do not need to return most of the May payment—you are just not entitled to the June 1st payment.

If any payments are made by the *Social Security Administration* (SSA) after death, they must be returned. To avoid any problems, you should promptly notify the SSA of the death of a recipient. Sometimes the funeral home will take care of this for you.

If the payments are made directly into the decedent's bank account, you should notify the bank to return any amounts received after the date of death.

The form **NOTICE OF DEATH TO SOCIAL SECURITY ADMINISTRATION** should be sent to the local office. (see form 38, p.221.) You can get their address by calling their local office listed in the beginning of the phone book under "federal government."

Needing a Will

Some may question whether a will is even necessary for their situations. This chapter will explain what a will can and cannot do, to make it clear whether a will is right for you.

WHAT A WILL CAN DO

A will does many different things, depending on what a person's relationship is to the deceased.

Beneficiaries   A will allows you to decide who gets your property after your death. You can give specific personal items to certain persons, and choose which of your friends or relatives, if any, deserve a greater share of your estate. You can also leave gifts to schools and charities.

Executor   A will allows you to decide who will be in charge of handling your estate. The *executor* (also called a *personal representative* or *administrator*):

- ✪ gathers together all your assets and distributes them to the beneficiaries;

✪   hires attorneys or accountants if necessary; and,

✪   files any essential tax or probate forms.

With a will, you can provide that your executor does not have to post a surety bond with the court in order to serve. You can also give the executor the power to sell your property and take other actions without getting a court order.

Guardian

A will allows you to choose a guardian for your minor children. This avoids fights among relatives and allows you to select the best person to raise your children. You may also appoint separate guardians over your children and over their money.

Example:
You may appoint your sister as guardian over your children, and your father as guardian over their money. This way, a second person can keep an eye on how the children's money is being spent.

Protecting Heirs

You can set up a trust to provide that your property is not distributed immediately. Many people feel that their children would not be ready to handle large sums of money at the age of majority (18 in most states). A will can direct that the money is held until the children are 21, 25, or older.

Minimizing Taxes

If your estate is over $2,000,000 (this amount will rise to $3,500,000 by 2009), it will be subject to federal estate taxes. If you wish to lower those taxes (by making gifts to charities, for example), you can do so through a will. However, such estate planning is beyond the scope of this book, and you should consult an estate planning attorney or another book for further information.

IF YOU HAVE NO WILL

If you do not have a will, the *intestacy* laws of your state determine who gets your property. As explained earlier, any property you owned in joint tenancy would automatically go to the joint owner, and any property held in trust would go to the beneficiaries (subject to the spouse's share in some states). But any property in your name alone would go to the persons named in your state's laws.

Each state's laws are different, but typically they provide as follows.

- ✪ If you have a spouse and children, the property is divided among them.

- ✪ If you have a spouse and parents or siblings, but no children, some states give all to your spouse, but other states give your parents or siblings a share.

- ✪ If you have children but no spouse, your children would get your property.

- ✪ If you have no children or spouse, your parents would get your property, except in a few states, which give a share to your brothers and sisters.

- ✪ If you have no spouse, children, or parents, your brothers and sisters would share your property.

- ✪ If you have no spouse, children, parents, brothers, or sisters, your property would go to your grandparents, aunts and uncles, or nieces and nephews, in that order.

Keep in mind that the above are general rules and some states have slight variations on these distributions.

MOVING TO ANOTHER STATE

A will that is valid in one state would probably be valid to pass property in another state. If your will is *self-proved*, as explained in Chapter 3, it might be admitted to probate without delay. However, if the will is not self-proved, then the witnesses to your will would need to be found and their oath taken to validate your will. In some states, a person would need to be appointed to take the oath of the witness, which would add to the time and expense of probating your will. It is advisable to execute a new will upon moving to another state.

Another advantage to having a new will is that it may help you avoid estate taxes in your former state.

Example:

George and Barbara left their high-tax state and retired to Florida, which has no estate or inheritance taxes, but they never made a new will. Upon their deaths, their former state of residence tried to collect a tax from their estate because their old wills stated that they were residents of that state.

WHO MAKES A WILL

In most states, any person who is 18 or more years of age and of sound mind may make a will. However, in Georgia and Puerto Rico the age is 14, and in Louisiana, the age is 16. In many states, a person who is married or in the armed forces is allowed to make a will, even if he or she is under the legal age. If you are underage and wish to make a will, you should check with an attorney.

WHAT A WILL CANNOT DO

A will cannot direct that anything illegal be done or put unreasonable conditions on a gift. A provision that your daughter gets all of your property if she divorces her husband will be ignored by the court. She will get the property with no conditions attached. You can put some conditions in your will. Consult with an attorney to be sure they are enforceable.

A will cannot leave money or property to an animal because animals cannot legally own property. If you wish to continue paying for care of an animal after your death, you should leave the funds in trust or to a friend you know will care for the animal.

WHO CAN USE A SIMPLE WILL

The wills in this book will pass your property whether your estate is $1,000 or $100,000,000. However, if your estate is over $2,000,000 (this amount will rise to $3,500,000 by 2009), you might be able to avoid estate taxes by using a trust or other tax-saving device. The larger your estate, the more you can save on estate taxes by doing more complicated planning. If you have a large estate and are concerned about estate taxes, you should consult an estate planning attorney or a book on estate planning.

WHO SHOULD NOT USE A SIMPLE WILL

If you expect that there may be a fight over your estate or that someone might contest your will's validity, you should consult a lawyer. If you leave less than the statutory share of your estate to your spouse or if you leave one or more of your children out of your will, it is likely that someone will contest your will. Other situations when you should not use a simple will include the following.

Complicated Estates

If you are the beneficiary of a trust or have any complications in your legal relationships, you may need special provisions in your will.

Blind or Unable to Write

A person who is blind or who can sign only with an "X" should also consult a lawyer about the proper way to make and execute a will.

Estates Over $2,000,000

If you expect to have over $2,000,000 (this amount will rise to $3,5000,000 by 2009) at the time of your death, then as discussed in the last section, you may want to consult with a certified public accountant (CPA) or tax attorney regarding tax consequences.

Conditions

If you wish to put conditions or restrictions on the property you leave, you should consult a lawyer.

Example:

If you want to leave money to your brother only if he quits smoking, or to a hospital only if they name a wing in your honor, you should consult an attorney to be sure that your conditions are valid in your state.

Making a Simple Will

If you have decided to use a will, this chapter will help you make one. You must know what property you are leaving to whom, and make sure everything you own gets addressed in your will.

IDENTIFYING PARTIES IN YOUR WILL

The first thing you must understand is who will be involved or connected to your will.

People When making your will, it is important to clearly identify the persons you name as your beneficiaries. In some families, names differ only by middle initial or by Jr. or Sr. Be sure to check everyone's name before making your will. You can also add your relationship to the beneficiary and their location, such as "my cousin, George Simpson of Clearwater, Florida."

Organizations Clarify the names of organizations and charities. For example, there is more than one group using the words "cancer society" or "heart association" in their name. Be sure to get the correct name of the group to which you intend to leave your gift.

Spouse and Children   In most states, you must mention your spouse and children in your will, even if you do not leave them any property. This is to show that you are of sound mind and know your heirs. As mentioned earlier, if you have a spouse or children and plan to leave your property to persons other than them, you should consult an attorney to be sure that your will is enforceable.

PERSONAL PROPERTY

Because people acquire and dispose of personal property so often, it is not advisable to list a lot of small items in your will. Otherwise, when you sell or replace one of them, you may have to rewrite your will.

One solution is to describe the type of item you wish to give.

Example:

Instead of saying, "I leave my 1998 Ford to my sister," state, "I leave any automobile I own at the time of my death to my sister."

Of course, if you do mean to give a specific item, you should describe it.

Example:

Rather than "I leave my diamond ring to Joan," you should say, "I leave to Joan the one-half carat diamond ring that I inherited from my grandmother," because you might own more than one diamond ring at the time of your death.

Handwritten List of Personal Property   In some states, you are allowed to leave a handwritten list of personal items you wish to go to certain people that would be legally binding. The states that allow this are listed in Appendix A. If your state is listed, you should make a handwritten list prior to making your will, sign and date it, and include the following statement under the "Specific Bequests" clause of your will.

I may leave a statement or list disposing of certain items of my tangible personal property. Any such statement or list in existence at the time of my death shall be determinative with respect to all items bequeathed therein.

A handwritten note is not an option in most states. If you feel your family will honor your wishes, you can write out a list of personal items you want to go to certain people, but you must realize that there is no legal requirement for your list to be followed.

NOTE: *Section 663 of the Internal Revenue Code allows the exclusion of certain specific bequests of tangible personal property from the estate. If your estate is over $2,000,000 (rising to $3,500,000 by 2009), you may want to consult a tax advisor about taking advantage of this provision.*

SPECIFIC BEQUESTS

Occasionally, a person will want to leave a little something to a friend or charity, and the rest to the family. This can be done with a *specific bequest*, such as, "$1,000 to my dear friend Martha Jones." There could be a problem if, at the time of a person's death, there was not anything left after the specific bequests.

Example:

At the time of making his will, Todd had $2,000,000 in assets. He felt generous, so he left $50,000 to a local hospital, $50,000 to a local group that took care of homeless animals, and the rest to his children. Unfortunately, several years later, the stock market crashed and he committed suicide by jumping off a bridge. His estate at the time was worth only $110,000, so after the specific bequests, and the legal fees and expenses of probate, there was nothing left for his five children.

Another problem with specific bequests is that some of the property may be worth considerably more or less at death than when the will was made.

Example:

Joe wanted his two children to equally share his estate. His will left his son his stocks (worth $500,000 at the time) and his daughter $500,000 in cash. By the time of Joe's death the stock was only worth $100,000. He should have left 50% of his estate to each child.

NOTE: *If giving certain things to certain people is an important part of your estate plan, you can give specific items to specific persons, but remember to make changes if your assets change.*

Joint Bequest

Be careful about leaving one item of personal property to more than one person. Whenever possible, leave property to one person.

Example:

If you leave something to your son and his wife, what would happen if they divorce? Even if you leave something to two of your own children, what if they cannot agree about who will have possession of it?

REMAINDER CLAUSE

One of the most important clauses in a will is the *remainder clause* (called a *residue clause* in some states). This is the clause that says something like, "all the rest, residue, and remainder of my property I leave to…" This clause makes sure that the will disposes of all property owned at the time of death and that nothing is forgotten.

In a simple will, the best way to distribute property is to put it all in the remainder clause. In the first example in the previous section, the problem would have been avoided if the will had read as follows: "The rest, residue, and remainder of my estate I leave 5% to ABC Hospital, 5% to XYZ Animal Welfare League, and 90% to be divided equally among my children…"

ALTERNATE BENEFICIARIES

You should always provide for an *alternate beneficiary* in case the first one dies before you and there is no chance for you to make out a new will.

Survivors or Descendants

Suppose your will leaves your property to your sister and brother, but your brother predeceases you. Should his share go to your sister or to your brother's children or grandchildren?

If you are giving property to two or more persons and you want it all to go to the other if one of them dies, then you would specify "or the survivor of them."

In Puerto Rico, you should clearly spell out whom you wish to receive your property. For example, if you leave property to your brother and wish for his children to receive it if he predeceases you, you should say, "to my brother, Jose Santiago, but if he predeceases me, to his children, Maria Santiago and Juan Santiago."

If, on the other hand, you want the property to go to the children of the deceased person, you should state in your will, "or their lineal descendants." This would include his or her children and grandchildren.

Family or Person

If you decide you want your estate to go to your brother's children and grandchildren, you must next decide if an equal share should go to each family or to each person.

Example:

If your brother leaves three grandchildren, and one is an only child of his daughter and the others are the children of his son, should all grandchildren get equal shares, or should they take their parent's share?

When you want each family to get an equal share, it is called *per stirpes*. When you want each person to get an equal share, it is called *per capita*. Most of the wills in this book use per stirpes because that is the most common way property is left. If you wish to leave your property per capita, then you can rewrite the will with this change.

Example 2:

Alice leaves her property to her two daughters, Mary and Pat, in equal shares, or to their lineal descendants per stirpes. Both daughters die before Alice. Mary leaves one child; Pat leaves two children. In this case, Mary's child would get half of the estate and Pat's children would split the other half of the estate. If Alice had specified per capita instead of per stirpes, each child would have gotten one-third of the estate.

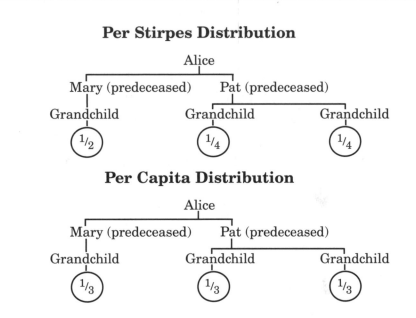

Per Stirpes Distribution

Alice
Mary (predeceased)   Pat (predeceased)
Grandchild   Grandchild   Grandchild
  $1/2$ $1/4$ $1/4$

Per Capita Distribution

Alice
Mary (predeceased)   Pat (predeceased)
Grandchild   Grandchild   Grandchild
  $1/3$ $1/3$ $1/3$

There are fourteen different will forms in Appendix C that cover most options, but you may want to divide your property slightly differently from what is stated in these forms. If so, you can retype the forms, specifying whether the property should go to the survivor or the lineal descendants. Consider seeking the advice of an attorney if you choose to retype the forms.

SURVIVORSHIP

Many people put a clause in their will stating that anyone receiving property under the will must survive for thirty days (or forty-five or sixty) after the death of the person who made the will. This is so if two people die in the same accident, there will not be two probates and the property will not go to the other party's heirs.

Example:

Fred and Wilma were married and each had children by previous marriages. They did not have survivorship clauses in their wills, and they were in an airplane crash and died. Fred's children hired several expert witnesses and a large law firm to prove that at the time of the crash Fred lived for a few minutes longer than Wilma. That way, when Wilma died first, all of her property went to Fred. When he died a few minutes later, all of Fred and Wilma's property went to his children. Wilma's children got nothing.

GUARDIANS

If you have minor children, you should name a *guardian* for them. There are two types of guardians—a guardian over the *person* and a guardian over the *property*. The first is the person who decides where the children will live and makes other parental decisions for them. A guardian of the property is in charge of the minor's property and inheritance. In most cases, one person is appointed guardian of both the person and property. However, some people prefer that the children live with one person and the money be held by another person.

Example:

Sandra was a widow with a young daughter. She knew that if anything happened to her, her sister would be the best person to raise her daughter. However, her sister was never good with money. When Sandra made out her will, she named her sister as guardian over the person of her daughter and she named her father as guardian over the estate of her daughter.

NOTE: *When naming a guardian, it is always advisable to name an alternate guardian in case your first choice is unable to serve for any reason.*

CHILDREN'S TRUST

When a parent dies, leaving a minor child, and the child's property is held by a guardian, the guardianship ends when the child reaches the age of 18, and all of the property is turned over to the child. Most parents do not feel their children are competent at the age of 18 to handle large sums of money, and prefer that it be held until they turn 21, 25, 30, or even older.

If you wish to set up a complicated system of determining when your children should receive various amounts of your estate, or if you want the property held to a higher age than 35, you should consult a lawyer to draft a trust. If instead you want a simple provision for the funds to be held until they reach an age older than 18, and you have someone you trust to make decisions about paying children's expenses, you can create a *Children's Trust*.

The Children's Trust trustee can be the same person as the guardian or a different person. It is advisable to name an alternate trustee if your first choice is unable to serve.

EXECUTOR OR PERSONAL REPRESENTATIVE

An *executor* (also called *personal representative* or *administrator* in some states) is the person who will be in charge of your probate. He or she will:

- gather your assets;

- handle the sale of your assets, if necessary;

- prepare an inventory;

- hire an attorney; and,

- distribute the property.

This should be a person you trust, and if it is, state in your will that no bond will be required to be posted by him or her. Otherwise, the court will require that a surety bond be paid for by your estate to guarantee that the person is honest. It is best to appoint a resident of your state as executor, because a bond may be required of a nonresident even if your will waives it.

Some individuals select two people to handle the estate to avoid jealousy, or to have them check on each other's honesty. However, this is not always a good idea. It makes double work in getting the papers signed, and there can be problems if they cannot agree on something.

A bank can serve as executor of your estate, but their fees are usually very high. Remember, the person handling your estate is usually entitled to some compensation. Some states specify a percentage, while others allow an hourly fee. A family member will often waive the fee. If there is a lot of work involved, the executor may request the fee, or other family members may insist that he or she take one. You can insist in your will that your executor or personal representative be paid a fee.

In most states, an executor or personal representative cannot sell your real estate without approval by the court. If you trust your executor, you can avoid the expense and delay of this by giving him or her the power to do so without court approval.

WITNESSES

A will must be *witnessed* by two persons to be valid in all states except Vermont, which requires three witnesses. In Puerto Rico, a will must be witnessed by either three or five persons, depending on the type of will. (See the section entitled "Puerto Rico" later in this chapter.) Each state has its own rule as to who can be a competent witness. While some states allow minors to witness wills, you should be sure that both of your witnesses are over 18 just to be safe.

The witnesses should not be people who are beneficiaries of your will. In about half the states, the witnesses *can* be beneficiaries, but it is better if they are not in case a question of undue influence arises.

SELF-PROVED AFFIDAVIT

It is highly recommended in most states that you include a notarized *self-proved* affidavit to the will. This is usually a separate sheet of paper attached to your will that is signed and *notarized* (sworn to under oath) at the same time your will is signed and witnessed.

If a will is accompanied by a notarized **SELF-PROVED WILL AFFIDAVIT**, it may be admitted to probate without delay or further contacting the witnesses. (see forms 17 and 18, p.179 and 181.)

Without a **SELF-PROVED WILL AFFIDAVIT**, your will cannot be admitted to probate until the court determines that it is valid. This can mean the witnesses must be located and asked to sign an oath, or if the witnesses are dead, someone may have to verify your handwriting.

The list on the following page will tell you whether you can use a **SELF-PROVED WILL AFFIDAVIT**, and if so, which one to use.

NOTE: *California, the District of Columbia, Michigan, and Wisconsin do not need to use these forms, and Ohio and Vermont do not provide for them.*

You are not required to have your will notarized—it just makes the probate process faster and easier. If it is difficult for you to get to a notary and you wish to make out your will right away, you can do so without a notary.

Alabama	form 17	Montana	form 17
Alaska	form 17	Nebraska	form 17
Arizona	form 17	Nevada	form 17
Arkansas	form 17	New Hampshire	form 20
California	Not necessary	New Jersey	form 18
Colorado	form 17	New Mexico	form 17
Connecticut	form 17	New York	form 17
Delaware	form 18	North Carolina	form 18
D.C.	Not necessary	North Dakota	form 17
Florida	form 18	Ohio	Not available
Georgia	form 18	Oklahoma	form 18
Hawaii	form 17	Oregon	form 17
Idaho	form 17	Pennsylvania	form 18
Illinois	form 17	Puerto Rico	Not available
Indiana	form 17	Rhode Island	form 18
Iowa	form 18	South Carolina	form 17
Kansas	form 18	South Dakota	form 17
Kentucky	form 18	Tennessee	form 17
Louisiana	form 19	Texas	form 21
Maine	form 17	Utah	form 17
Maryland	Not necessary	Vermont	Not available
Massachusetts	form 18	Virginia	form 18
Michigan	Not necessary	Washington	form 17
Minnesota	form 17	West Virginia	form 17
Mississippi	form 17	Wisconsin	Not necessary
Missouri	form 18	Wyoming	form 18

DISINHERITING SOMEONE

Do not make your own will if you intend to disinherit someone, because it may result in your will being challenged in court. However, you may wish to leave one child less than another because you already made a gift to that child, or perhaps that because child needs the money less than the other.

If you do give more to one child than to another, then you should state your reasons, in order to show that you thought out your plan. Otherwise, the one who received less might argue that you did not realize what you were doing and were not competent to make a will.

In Puerto Rico, you cannot disinherit your children unless you have a *good legal reason*. Examples include a child refusing to support you or abusing you grievously by words. If you wish to disinherit a child in Puerto Rico, you should seek the advice of a *notary*. In the fifty states, a notary public merely administers oaths and confirms the identity of someone signing a document. However, a notary public in Puerto Rico is like an attorney in private practice, and can draft wills and other legal documents.

Your living parents are entitled to one-half of your estate if you have no children, as mentioned earlier. You cannot disinherit them without good legal reason, either. Examples of good legal reason include if they accused you of a crime or failed to furnish your bail when they could have done so. Consult a notary if you wish to disinherit your parents.

FUNERAL ARRANGEMENTS

There is no harm in stating your preferences in your will, but in most states, directions for a funeral are not legally enforceable. A will is often not found until after the funeral. Therefore, it is better to tell your family about your wishes or to make prior arrangements yourself.

HANDWRITTEN WILLS

In some states and Puerto Rico, you can hand write your own will, without any witnesses, and it will be held valid. This is called a *holographic will*. As a general rule, it must be completely written in your own handwriting, dated, and signed, and it must clearly express your intention to make it your will. It is only valid in the states listed in Appendix A.

Since there is a greater chance it may be held invalid for some reason, a holographic will should only be used if you are in an emergency situation and are unable to find anyone to sign as witnesses.

In Puerto Rico, a holographic will is the only kind of will you can make without the services of a notary.

LOUISIANA

Louisiana's legal system is different from all forty-nine other states because it is based on the French system rather than the English.

Under Louisiana law, there are two types of wills. The original will law required a will to be transcribed by a notary and witnessed by three persons (five if they did not reside locally), and it had to strictly follow certain formalities.

Recently, Louisiana passed a statutory will law that is similar to most other states. A statutory will needs only two witnesses but it *must be notarized* and *every page must be signed in full by the testator*. For Louisiana, Appendix C has a notary page (form 19, page 183.) instead of a self-proved will page. Also, since Louisiana has parishes rather than counties, the word "County" should be crossed out and replaced with the word "Parish."

PUERTO RICO

The legal system of Puerto Rico is also different from the rest of the United States because it is based upon the Spanish Civil Code. One big difference in the two systems is that in Puerto Rico, a notary public is nearly the equivalent of a lawyer in private practice, as described previously.

In Puerto Rico, there are three types of wills: holographic wills, closed wills, and open wills. A holographic will can be done without a notary, while open and closed wills must be formalized with the services of a notary.

Holographic Will

As defined before, a *holographic will* is a will that you write yourself, completely in your own handwriting. In Puerto Rico, it must have your signature and the month, day, and year that you signed it. It can only be made by persons of full age, and if it contains any words that are erased, corrected, or interlined, then you must make a note of this under your signature.

Closed Will

A *closed will* is one that is either written by you or by another person with your direction on common paper giving the place, day, month, and year. If you write it yourself, you must write at the top of each page that it is your last will and testament and sign at the end after mentioning any words erased, corrected, or interlined. If it is written by someone else, you should sign every page as well as at the end. A closed will must then be sealed in an envelope in the presence of a notary and five witnesses. The notary must draft a memorandum on the wrapper of the will and follow strict procedures to assure its validity.

Open Will

An *open will* is one that is executed before a notary and three witnesses after it is read aloud to them. In most cases, the notary will want to participate in the drafting of such a will. If a person is in imminent danger of death, the will may be executed before five witnesses without a notary. If the person does not die within two months, the will is void.

CAUTIONS

Your will should have no white-outs or erasure marks. If, for some reason, it is impossible to make a will without corrections, they should be initialed by you and both witnesses. The pages should be fastened together and they should state at the bottom, "page 1 of 3," "page 2 of 3," etc. If you are using a **SELF-PROVED WILL AFFIDAVIT** page or notary page, you should include this page in the numbering of the pages to be sure it is counted as part of your will. Each page should be initialed by you and by the witnesses.

Executing Your Will

The signing of a will is a serious legal event, and must be done properly or the will may be declared invalid. Preferably, it should be done in a private room without distraction. All parties must watch each other sign and no one should leave the scene until all have signed.

Example:

Ebenezer was bedridden in a small room. His will was brought in to him to sign, but the witnesses could not actually see his hand signing because a dresser was in the way. His will was ignored by the court and his property went to two people who were not in his will.

PROCEDURE

To be sure your will is valid, you should follow these rules:

❑   You must state to your witnesses: "This is my will. I have read it and I understand it and this is how I want it to read. I want you two (or three) people to be my witnesses." Contrary to popular belief, you do not have to read it to the witnesses or let them read it.

❑ You must date your will and sign your name at the end in ink exactly as it is printed in the will, and you should initial each page as the witnesses watch. In Louisiana, you must sign each page of the will with your full signature and have your will notarized.

❑ You and the other witnesses must watch as each witness signs in ink and initials each page.

SELF-PROVED WILL AFFIDAVIT

As explained in the last chapter, it is important to attach a self-proving affidavit to your will. This means you will need to have a notary public present to watch everyone sign. If it is impossible to have a notary present, your will is still valid (except in Louisiana), but the probate process may be delayed.

After your witnesses have signed as attesting witnesses under your name, you and they should sign the self-proving page and the notary should notarize it. The notary should not be one of your witnesses.

It is a good idea to make at least one copy of your will, but you should not personally sign the copies or have them notarized. If you cancel or destroy your will, someone may produce a copy and have it probated. Also, if you lose or destroy a copy, a court may assume you intended to revoke the original.

Example:

Michael typed out a copy of his will and made two photocopies. He had the original and both copies signed and notarized. He then gave the original to his sister, who was his executor, and kept the two copies. Upon his death, the two copies were not found among his papers. Because these copies were in his possession and not found, it was assumed that he destroyed them. A court ruled that by destroying them, he must have intended to revoke the original will and his property went to people not listed in his will.

In Puerto Rico, a notary must conduct the execution of a will and it must conform to the law without interruption. If a will is not valid because of a noncompliance with the law, the notary can be held liable.

After Signing Your Will

There are certain steps you should take after signing your will to ensure your will is found intact. Also, there are things you can do to change your will after you sign, as addressed in this chapter.

STORING YOUR WILL

Your will should be kept in a place safe from fire and easily accessible to your heirs. Your personal representative or executor should know of its whereabouts. It can be kept in a home safe or fire box.

In some states, the opening of a safe deposit box in a bank after a person's death is a complicated affair, so it is not advisable to keep it there.

If you are close to your children and can trust them explicitly, you could allow one of them to keep the will in his or her safe deposit box. However, if you later decide to limit that child's share, there could be a problem.

Example:

Diane made out her will giving her property to her two children equally and gave it to her oldest child, Bill, to hold. Years later, Bill moved away and her youngest child, Mary, took care of her by coming over every day. Diane made a new will giving most of her property to Mary. Upon Diane's death, Bill came to town and found the new will in Diane's house, but he destroyed it and probated the old will, which gave him half the property.

In some states, a will can be filed with the probate division of the local court system. This can be a good way to be sure your will is not lost. However, if you ever want to revoke your will while in the hospital, it could make things more difficult.

Puerto Rico   In Puerto Rico, if you have a closed will, you cannot open the sealed envelope or it will be presumed that the will is revoked. It is even possible it will be revoked if someone else opens it, or if there is a tear in any way in the outer wrapper. Therefore, you should consider having your will held by a person you can trust, such as the notary who authenticated it.

REVOKING YOUR WILL

The most common way to revoke a will is to execute a new one that states an intent to revoke all previously made wills. To revoke a will without making a new one, tear, burn, cancel, deface, obliterate, or destroy it. This must be done with the intention of revoking it, and not done accidentally. If accidental, the will is not legally revoked.

Example:

Ralph tells his son Clyde to go to the basement safe and tear up his (Ralph's) will. If Clyde does not tear it up in Ralph's presence, it is probably not effectively revoked.

Revival What if you change your will by drafting a new one but later decide you do not like the changes and want to go back to your old will? Can you destroy the new one and revive (bring back) the old one? Once you execute a new will revoking an old will, you cannot revive the old will unless you execute a new document stating that you intend to revive the old will. In other words, you must execute a new will.

In Puerto Rico, the law is different. You can revive an old will by revoking a newer will and making clear your intent. However, it is usually best to execute a new will to avoid any misunderstanding.

CHANGING YOUR WILL

You should not make any changes on your will after it has been signed. If you cross out a person's name or add a clause, your change will not be valid and your entire will might become invalid.

One way to amend a will is to execute a *codicil*. A codicil is an amendment to a will. However, a codicil must be executed just like a will. It must have the same number of witnesses, and include a self-proving page that must be notarized.

NOTE: *As a codicil requires the same formality as a will, it may be better to make a new will.*

If you want to change something in your will, but cannot get to a notary to have it self-proved, you can execute a codicil that is witnessed, but not self-proved. As long as it is properly witnessed (two witnesses in all states except Vermont, which requires three), it will legally change your will. The witnesses will have to later sign an oath if the codicil was not self-proved.

To prepare a codicil in any state except Louisiana, use form 22. To self-prove the codicil, use forms 23, 24, or 25. (See page 35 for a list of which form to use for which state.)

Making a Living Will

A **LIVING WILL** has nothing to do with the usual type of will that distributes property. A *living will* is a document by which a person declares that he or she does not want artificial life support systems used if he or she becomes terminally ill.

Modern science can often keep a body alive even if the brain is permanently dead, or if the person is in constant pain. In recent years, all states have legalized living wills either by statute or by court decision. Some states have suggested forms and others allow any writing that reasonably expresses a person's wishes.

A **LIVING WILL** must be signed in front of two witnesses who should not be blood relatives or a spouse. If the person is physically unable to sign, he or she may read the **LIVING WILL** out loud and direct one of the witnesses to sign it for him or her.

Form 26 is a **LIVING WILL** form that complies with the law in every state. However, some doctors are more comfortable with the form designed for their state, even if it is not required. If you wish to use your state's form, you can probably get one from your doctor or hospital.

Making Powers of Attorney

A *power of attorney* is a document that gives someone the right to take some legal action in your name. For example, you might give someone a power of attorney to sign a deed selling your house if you are going to be out of the country. You could also give someone power of attorney to handle all of your legal affairs in case you were medically disabled.

A person holding a power of attorney to act for someone is called an *attorney in fact*. (This has no relationship to an *attorney at law*.) The person giving someone a power of attorney is called the *grantor*. While an attorney in fact should only take action that the grantor wishes, he or she has the *power* to do anything that the power of attorney grants. For example, an attorney in fact can withdraw money from a grantor's account and spend it for personal gain. (Of course, this would be criminal.)

For this reason, a power of attorney should only be given to a trusted person. It should be limited to necessary acts. For example, if you need someone to sign a real estate deed, it is not necessary to give them a **GENERAL POWER OF ATTORNEY** allowing them to do anything regarding all of your property. (see form 27, p.199.) Instead, you would give them a **SPECIFIC POWER OF ATTORNEY** for the specific act of signing the deed. (see form 28, p.201.) A sample of a **SPECIFIC POWER OF ATTORNEY** is below.

POWER OF ATTORNEY—SPECIFIC

_____Robert Smith_____ (the "Grantor") hereby grants to _____Lois Smith_____ (the "Agent") a limited power of attorney. As the Grantor's attorney in fact, the Agent shall have full power and authority to undertake and perform the following on behalf of the Grantor:

By accepting this grant, the Agent agrees to act in a fiduciary capacity consistent with the reasonable best interests of the Grantor. This power of attorney may be revoked by the Grantor at any time; however, any person dealing with the Agent as attorney in fact may rely on this appointment until receipt of actual notice of termination.

IN WITNESS WHEREOF, the undersigned grantor has executed this power of attorney under seal as of the date stated above.

There may be times when you have given someone a power of attorney and then later decide to cancel it. This is done with a form called a **REVOCATION OF POWER OF ATTORNEY**. (see form 29, p.203.) You should deliver it to the person with the power of attorney as well as anyone you think has seen or will see the original power of attorney.

HEALTH CARE POWER OF ATTORNEY

When you enter a hospital, you never know if you will be able to make all the judgment calls necessary throughout your treatment. To solve this, in most states you can sign a **HEALTH CARE POWER OF ATTORNEY**, which allows someone else to make decisions for you.

The form included in this book is a generic one. If your hospital has its own form, you should use that one. If there is no other form available, you can use this one and check with your hospital to see if they will honor it. (see form 30, p.205.)

Making Anatomical Gifts

Residents of all states are allowed to donate their bodies or organs for research or transplantation. Consent may be given by a relative of a deceased person, but because relatives are often in shock or too upset to make such a decision, it is better to have one's intent made clear before death. This can be done by a statement in a will or by another signed document, such as a **UNIFORM DONOR CARD**. (see form 31, p.207.). The gift may be of all or part of one's body, and it may be made to a specific person, such as a physician or an ill relative.

The document making the donation must be signed before two witnesses, who must also sign in each other's presence. If the donor cannot sign, then the document may be signed for him or her at his or her direction in the presence of the witnesses.

The donor may designate in the document who the physician is that will carry out the procedure.

If the document or will has been delivered to a specific donee, it may be amended or revoked by the donor in the following ways:

- ✪ by executing and delivering a signed statement to the donee;

- ✪ by an oral statement to two witnesses communicated to the donee;

- ✪ by an oral statement made to an attending physician during a terminal illness and communicated to the donee; or,

- ✪ by a signed document found on the person of the donor or in his or her effects.

If a document of gift has not been delivered to a donee, it may be revoked by any of the above methods or by destruction, cancellation, or mutilation of the document. It may also be revoked in the same method a will is revoked as described on page 46.

Making an Ethical Will

A Last Will and Testament allows you to distribute the material wealth you have accumulated in your lifetime. But you most likely have also accumulated a lot of practical, intellectual, and spiritual wealth, and it is possible to share that with your family as well.

An *ethical will* is a message to one's children or heirs in which you share your thoughts, advice, and wisdom. It is not legally binding, but it allows you to pass on something that may be worth more than the money and property you leave.

People have written ethical wills for thousands of years, but more people are starting to write them now. A sample ethical will is included in Appendix B.

ITEMS INCLUDED

Some of the things people have put in their ethical wills are:

- ✪ explanations of why they left their property as they did;

- ✪ lessons they learned during their life;

- beliefs they have found to be true in life;

- advice they wish to leave their children or grandchildren;

- requests that people grieve, but enjoy life;

- acknowledgement of love for family members;

- forgiveness to those who hurt them;

- requests for forgiveness from those they hurt;

- special stories or anecdotes from their life; and,

- family history that should be passed on.

USES

An ethical will should not be used to get even with people, to try to cause guilt, or say anything too outlandish. If someone is not happy with your *legal* will (the one giving away property), he or she may use your unusual ethical will to argue that you were not competent to make a will. If a judge agrees with him or her, your *legal* will could be thrown out.

The ethical will is not only a message to others—it is a framework for gathering your thoughts and contemplating your past and your future. There are many points in a person's life when he or she might consider writing an ethical will. Some of them are:

- upon becoming engaged or married;

- upon the birth of a new child;

- at the death of a parent or grandparent;

- at retirement; or,

- near the end of life.

FORMAT

An ethical will can be anything from a short, handwritten note to a long videotape. Some people put together a book and include photographs. Others put it all on a diskette or CD-ROM.

When using some sort of technology to make your ethical will, remember that by the time you die, certain formats may be obsolete. If you leave a videotape or diskette, your family might not have a machine that can read it twenty or thirty years from now. If you do not update it to new formats over the years, at least try to leave a hard copy as well as a digital copy.

Avoiding Probate

Everyone who knows what probate is wants to avoid it. As stated earlier, probate is the determination that a will is valid and that the estate should be settled by the will's terms. It is often a long, arduous procedure. Luckily, the laws are changing to allow many different ways to avoid probate. This section explains the easiest ones. (For more detailed information, there are many books available that specifically discuss the probate process.)

JOINT PROPERTY

The easiest way to avoid probate is to own all property in *joint tenancy with right of survivorship*. When property is owned this way, it automatically passes to the survivor when the other owner dies. Three disadvantages of this are:

1. either owner can secretly take the property at any time;

2. either party's creditor's can take it; and,

3. if both parties die at the same time, there still has to be a probate.

To set up property in joint ownership, it must be titled with the names of both parties and the words:

as joint tenants with full rights of survivorship.

Merely putting two names on an account without this language does not mean the survivor gets it. This language can be on deeds of real estate, stock certificates, brokerage accounts, and bank accounts.

NOTE: *Some states allow married couples to jointly hold certain property (usually deeded property) as* **tenants by the entirety**. *This allows for an extra level of protection from creditors in states that allow it.*

Most married couples who jointly own all their property and want all of it to go to their spouse do not need a will when the first one of them dies. The main reason they *should* have one is in the event of an accident that kills both of them.

One solution to this problem is for a couple to put their property in joint ownership with their children. Possible dangers of this is that the children can take all of the property at any time, and the creditors of a child might be able to seize it. (The next subsections *Totten Trust* and *Formal Trust* describe solutions for this.)

You should review how your bank accounts, stocks, mutual funds, motor vehicles, recreation vehicles, and other property are titled. If you want them to go to your relatives or through your will, they should be in your name alone. If you want them to go to your joint owner, you should be sure they are properly set up as a joint account with right of survivorship.

TOTTEN TRUST

A *Totten Trust* can solve some of the problems of joint ownership. This is a method of setting up the title to property so that it automatically passes at death without the beneficiary having any rights to it until the first owner's life is over. It was named after the court case in which a court held that it was legal to do.

A Totten Trust is established when the property is set up in trust for (I/T/F), with a named beneficiary. Some institutions may use the letters POD for *pay on death* or TOD for *transfer on death*. Either way, the result is the same. No one, except you, can get the money until your death. Upon death, it immediately goes directly to the person you name, without a will or probate proceeding.

Totten Trusts have been valid for a long time for bank accounts. During the last decade, more than half the states have passed laws allowing them to be used for securities such as stocks, bonds, and mutual funds. They are not yet used for real estate, though in some states, the law seems to allow it. Check with a lawyer before attempting to use it for real estate.

If your financial advisor will not or cannot set up your mutual fund or brokerage account to pay on death, check with some others located in another state. Yours may be located in a state where the law has not passed.

FORMAL TRUST

Another way to avoid needing a will (and to avoid probate) is to set up a Formal Trust. A trust is an agreement in which someone holds property that really belongs to someone else. It is then used for the latter person's benefit. For example, a person might transfer all his or her stocks to a bank to hold in trust. The trust would provide that during that person's life, he or she gets all the dividends from the stock. Then, after his or her death, the income goes to the children.

If the trust is *revocable*, the person setting up the trust (the *settlor*) can change the trust or even dissolve it. If it is *irrevocable*, it cannot be changed. The benefit of a revocable trust is that no one else can get to it, meaning if you or your children later have a large liability (medical bills or liability for an accident), the creditors cannot touch the money in the trust (if it is set up correctly).

A **LIVING TRUST**, often called a *Revocable Living Trust* or an *Inter Vivos Trust*, is usually a trust that a person or couple sets up in which they become their own trustees. The main benefit of this is that their property then avoids probate. (see form 32, p.209.)

There are many other benefits of trusts. The laws differ from state to state as to the legal requirements; for example, whether a person can be his or her own trustee. (A thorough discussion is beyond the scope of this book; however, if you think a living trust could benefit you, consult a book on living trusts.)

PERSONAL PROPERTY

One of the biggest problems with setting up a living trust is that people forget to put their property into it. After the trust agreement is signed, all of the person's property must be transferred to the trust. Usually, all of the assets are listed on a **SCHEDULE OF ASSETS** that goes with the trust. A form for this is included in Appendix C. (see form 33, p.211.) But for some types of property, such as real estate and motor vehicles, the title must be reregistered. This means getting a new deed or title certificate. Also, bank and brokerage accounts must be retitled, rather than just listed on the **SCHEDULE OF ASSETS**.

Personal property ownership is not registered or documented by a title certificate. As a result, ownership of such items can be questionable. For example, what if you own a valuable coin collection, and after your death, your spouse claims ownership as joint property, while your child claims inheritance as personal property under your will?

To avoid problems like this, you can specifically list personal items you wish to give people in your will. You can sign a declaration with your spouse or partner as to how your personal property is titled. A **DECLARATION OF JOINT PROPERTY** can help do this. (see form 34, p.213.) An example of such a form in on the next page.

DECLARATION OF JOINT PROPERTY

The undersigned, in consideration of the mutual agreement herein contained, agree that all property owned by them and located in their place of residence, shall be owned in joint tenancy with full rights of survivorship, except the following items which shall remain separate property for all purposes:

Except John Smith's coin collection, which will be willed to his son.

Except Mildred Smith's family photo album, which will be willed to her sister's children.

In addition to the property located at the residence, the following property shall also be owned in joint tenancy with full rights of survivorship:

John Smith's canoe, which is usually kept by the river.

In witness whereof, the parties affix their signatures and seals this ___29th___ day of _____January_____, 20_06_.

In some cases, you might be more concerned that the title to your property is separate. For example, in California and many other western states, all property acquired during marriage is considered *community property*, and each spouse has 50% interest in it. If you and your spouse want to keep your property separate (for example, to leave it to your separate children), you could execute a **DECLARATION OF SEPARATE PROPERTY**. (see form 35, p.215.)

Amendments and Termination

If a living trust needs to be changed (such as when one beneficiary dies), this is done with an **AMENDMENT**. (see form 36, p.217.) A **TERMINATION** form to end the trust is also included. (see form 37, p.219.)

Glossary

A

administrator. A person appointed by a court to manage a person's state (for example, if no executor was named).

B

beneficiary. A person who is left property in a will.

bequeath. To leave someone personal property in a will.

bequest. A gift of personal property in a will.

C

codicil. An amendment to a will.

D

decedent. The person who has died.

descendant. A living child, grandchild, great-grandchild, etc. of the person who has died.

devise. A gift of real property in a will; also, to leave real property in a will.

devisee. A person who is left real property in a will.

E

elective share. The amount of property a spouse can claim even if nothing was left to him or her in the will.

ethical will. A message to one's children or heirs in which one shares one's thoughts, advice, and wisdom.

executor. A person appointed in a will to manage a decedent's estate. In some states, this person is now called a *personal representative*.

exempt property. Property regularly used by decedent's family and that is not considered part of the estate.

F

family allowance. An amount allowed by law to the spouse and children of a decedent.

forced share. *See elective share.*

G

guardian. A person appointed by a court to have legal control over a minor's person or property.

H

heir. A person who inherits property from a person without a will.

homestead. In some states, the residence of a person who is married or has minor children.

I

intestate. The state of dying without a valid will.

intestate share. The amount of property an heir receives from the estate of a person who died without a will.

I/T/F. Abbreviation that stands for "in trust for." This is a way to keep bank accounts out of an estate.

J

joint tenancy. Ownership of property in which, upon death, an owner's share goes to the other joint owner.

joint tenancy with right of survivorship. *See joint tenancy.*

L

legacy. A gift of personal property in a will.

legal will. *See will.*

living will. A document that directs medical personnel whether or not to use extraordinary measures to keep a body alive after certain life functions have ceased.

N

notary. An official authorized to administer oaths.

notary public. In the fifty states—a public officer who can administer oaths and confirm the identity of a person signing a document. In Puerto Rico—a public officer who can prepare wills and other legal documents.

P

personal representative. A person appointed in a will to manage a decedent's estate. In some states, this person is now called an *executor*.

POD (also P/O/D). Pay on death, usually used on bank accounts and in some states on securities.

probate. The procedure of gathering a decedent's assets and distributing them to the heirs or beneficiaries.

R

remainder. Balance of any real property in an estate after all specific gifts have been distributed.

residue. Balance of an estate after all specific gifts have been distributed.

revival. When a legal document becomes enforceable again after being unenforceable for a time.

S

specific bequest. The gift of a specific item of personal property to a specific person in a will.

specific devise. The gift of a specific parcel of real property to a specific person in a will.

T

tenancy by the entireties. In some states, the ownership of property by a husband and wife as one entity. When one dies, the other still owns the entire property.

tenancy in common. Ownership of property in which, upon death, each owner's share goes to his or her heirs or beneficiaries.

testate. To be with a valid will, as in *a testate estate*.

testator. A person making a will.

TOD (also T/O/D). Transfer on death. Usually used on bank accounts and in some states on securities.

Totten Trust. Titling property "in trust for" another person, but that can be changed at any time before death.

W

will. A document you can use to control who gets specific property, who will be guardian of your children and their property, and who will manage your estate upon your death.

State Laws

Since the laws are different in each state, the following tables have been included to provide information about your specific state on matters discussed in the text. Keep in mind that laws are amended frequently and are subject to interpretation by the court.

Special thanks are due to Alexandra Schiller
for her work in updating all of the laws in this appendix.

SPOUSE'S ENTITLEMENT TO ESTATE

The following table is a summary of the share of an estate that a spouse is entitled to by law. When only a fraction or percentage is given the share is of the probatable estate. The word *augmented* is used to indicate all assets passing at death were used to calculate the share. Where the word *community* is used the state is a community property state. The spouse is entitled to one-half of all community property (most property acquired during the marriage). When it says "up to fifty percent," this is a sliding scale based on the length of the marriage.

Keep in mind that these are brief summaries and that the laws can change. If this is an issue in your estate planning, check the most recent version of your state statute or consult an attorney.

Alabama

Share: ⅓ augmented
Statute: Ala. Code Sec. 43-8-70

Alaska

Share: ⅓ augmented
Statute: Alaska Stat. Sec. 13.12.201–.214

Arizona

Share: ½ community
Statute: Ariz. Rev. Stat. Sec. 25-211, 14-3101

Arkansas

Share: ⅓ to ½ augmented
Statute: Ark. Code Ann. Sec. 28-39-401

California

Share: ½ community
Statute: Cal. Prob. Code Sec. 21610, 21611, 6401

Colorado

Share: 5% to 50% augmented
Statute: Colo. Rev. Stat. Sec. 15-11-201

Connecticut

Share: ¹/₃ for life
Statute: Conn. Gen. Stat. Sec. 45A-436

Delaware

Share: ¹/₃ augmented
Statute: Del. Code Ann. 12 Sec. 901–908

District of Columbia

Share: ¹/₃ up to ¹/₂
Statute: D.C. Code Ann. Sec. 19-113

Florida

Share: 30% augmented
Statute: Fla. Stat. Sec. 732.201, 732.2065

Georgia

Share: one year's support
Statute: Ga. Code Ann. Sec. 53-3-13

Hawaii

Share: up to 50% augmented
Statute: Haw. Rev. State Sec. 560:2-202

Idaho

Share: ¹/₂ augmented quasi-community
Statute: Idaho Code Sec. 15-2-203

Illinois

Share: ½ if no children; ⅓ if children
Statute: 755 ILCS 5/2-8

Indiana

Share: ½ if no children; ⅓ if children
Statute: Ind. Code Ann. Sec. 29-1-3-1

Iowa

Share: ⅓ plus all exempt
Statute: Iowa Code Ann. Sec. 633.238

Kansas

Share: up to 50% augmented
Statute: Kan. Stat. Ann. Sec. 59-6a202

Kentucky

Share: ½ personal property; ½ real estate
Statute: Ky. Rev. Stat. Ann. Sec. 392.020, 392.080

Louisiana

Share: ½ community
Statute: La. Code. Ann. Art. 3001

Maine

Share: ⅓ augmented
Statute: Me. Rev. Stat. Ann.Tit 18a, Sec. 2-201

Maryland

Share: ½ if no children; ⅓ if children
Statute: Md. Code Ann. Est. & Trusts Sec. 3-203

Massachusetts
Share: $25k plus ½ without children; ⅓ if children
Statute: Mass. Ann. Laws Ch.191 Sec. 15

Michigan
Share: ½ of intestate
Statute: Mich. Stat. Ann. Sec. 27.5282;
            Mich. Comp. Laws Ann. Sec. 700.202

Minnesota
Share: up to 50%
Statute: Minn. Stat. Ann. Sec. 524.2-202

Mississippi
Share: ½
Statute: Miss. Code Ann. Sec. 91-1-7, 91-5-25, 915-27

Missouri
Share: ½ if no children; ⅓ if children
Statute: Mo. Ann. Stat. Sec. 474-160

Montana
Share: up to 50% augmented
Statute: Mont. Code Ann. Sec. 72-2-221

Nebraska
Share: ½ augmented
Statute: Neb. Rev. Stat. Sec. 30-2313

Nevada
Share: ½ community plus support
Statute: Nev. Rev. Stat. Sec. 46.010

New Hampshire

Share: ½ plus $10K without children; ⅓ if children
Statute: N. H. Rev. Stat. Ann. Sec. 560:10

New Jersey

Share: ⅓ augmented
Statute: N.J. Stat. Ann. Sec. 3B:8-1

New Mexico

Share: ½ community
Statute: N.M. Stat. Sec. 45-2A-6

New York

Share: ½ if no children; ⅓ if children
Statute: N.Y. Est. Powers & Trusts Law Sec. 5-1.1(c)

North Carolina

Share: ¼ to ½
Statute: N.C. Gen. Stat. Sec. 29-14, 30-3.1

North Dakota

Share: ½ augmented
Statute: N.D. Cent. Code Sec. 30.1-05-01

Ohio

Share: ½ if no or 1 child; ⅓ if 2 children
Statute: Ohio Rev. Code Ann. Sec. 2106.01

Oklahoma

Share: ½ marital property
Statute: Okla. Stat. Ann. Tit. 84 Sec. 44

Oregon

Share: ½ community

Statute: Or. Rev. Stat. Sec.112.705–.775

Pennsylvania

Share: ⅓ augmented

Statute: 20 PA. Cons. Stat. Ann. Sec. 2203

Puerto Rico

Share: ½ plus life estate in children's share

Statute: P.R.C.C. Sec. 2411

Rhode Island

Share: ⅓ real estate for life plus $75,000

Statute: R.I. Gen. Laws Sec. 33-1-6, 33-25-2

South Carolina

Share: ½ intestate estate

Statute: S.C. Code Ann. Sec. 62-2-201

South Dakota

Share: up to 50% augmented

Statute: S.D. Codified Laws Sec. 29A-2-202

Tennessee

Share: 10% to 40%

Statute: Tenn. Code Ann. Sec. 31-4-101

Texas

Share: ½ community

Statute: Tex. Prob. Code Ann. Sec. 15

Utah
Share: ⅓ augmented
Statute: Utah Code Ann. Sec. 75-2-202

Vermont
Share: ⅓ or more
Statute: VT. Stat. Ann. Tit. Sec. 401, 402

Virginia
Share: ½ if no children; ⅓ if children
Statute: VA. Code Ann. Sec. 64.1-16

Washington
Share: ½ community
Statute: Rev. Code of Wash. Sec. 11.02.070

West Virginia
Share: up to 50% augmented
Statute: W.Va. Code Sec. 42-3-1

Wisconsin
Share: ½ community
Statute: Wis. Stat. Sec. 861.01–.03

Wyoming
Share: ½ if no children of prior spouse;
          ¼ if children of prior spouse
Statute: Wyo. Stat. Ann. Sec. 2-5-101

STATE STATUTES ALLOWING TRANSFERS AT DEATH OF SECURITIES

The following states allow securities to be registered in *transfer-on-death* form. If your state is listed you can ask that your stock and mutual fund accounts be set up in transfer-on-death format. (see pages 60–61).

If your state is not listed, check with your broker, lawyer, or state statutes to see if your state's law has changed recently, or you can move your accounts to a company in a state that has passed the law.

Alabama	Ala. Code Sec. 8-6-140 to 8-6-151
Alaska	Alaska Stat. Sec. 13.06.050, 13.33.301 to 13.33.310
Arizona	Ariz. Rev. Stat. Sec. 14-1201, 14-6301 to 14-6311
Arkansas	Ark. Code Ann. Sec. 28-14-101 to 28-14-112
California	Cal. Prob. Code Sec. 5500 to 5512
Colorado	Colo. Rev. Stat. Ann. Sec. 15-10-201, 15-15-301 to -311
Connecticut	Conn. Gen. Stat. Sec. 45a-468 to 45a-468m
Delaware	Del. Code Ann. 12 Sec. 801 to 812
Florida	Fla. Stat. Sec. 711.50 to 711.512
Georgia	Off. Code of Ga. Ann. Secs. 53-5-60 to 71
Hawaii	Haw. Rev. Stat. Sec. 539-1 to 539-12
Idaho	Idaho Code Sec. 15-6-301 to 16-6-312
Illinois	S.H.A. 815 Ill. Comp. Stat. 10/0.01 to 10/12
Indiana	Ind. Code Sec. 32-4-1.6-1 to 32-4-1.6-15
Iowa	Iowa Code Sec. 633.800 to 633.811
Kansas	Kan. Stat. Ann.17-49a 01 to 17-49a 12
Kentucky	Ky. Rev. Stat. Ann. Sec. 292.6501 to 292.6512
Maine	Me. Rev. Stat. Ann. 18A Sec. 6-301 to 6-312

Maryland	Md. Code Ann. Est. & Trusts, Sec. 16-101 to 16-112
Massachusetts	Mass. Gen. Laws. Ch. 201E, Sec. 101 to 402
Michigan	Mich. Comp. Laws Ann. Sec. 451.471 to 451.481
Minnesota	Minn. Stat. Ann. Sec. 542.1-201, 524.6-301 to 524.6-311
Mississippi	Miss. Code Ann. Sec. 91-21-1 to 91-21-25
Montana	Mont. Code Ann. Sec. 72-1-103, 72-6-301 to 72-6-311
Nebraska	Neb. Rev. Stat. 1943, Sec. 30-2209, 30-2734 to 30-2746
Nevada	Nev. Rev. Stat. Sec. 111.480 to 111.650
New Hampshire	N.H. Rev. Stat. Ann. Sec. 563-C:1 to 563-C:12
New Jersey	N.J. Stat. Ann. Sec. 3B:30-1 to3B:30-12
New Mexico	N.M.Stat. Ann. 1978, Sec. 45-1-201, 45-6-301 to 45-6-311
North Dakota	N.D. Cent. Code 30.1-01-06, 30.1-31-21 to 30.1-31-30
Ohio	Ohio Rev. Code Ann. Sec. 1709.01 to 1709.11
Oklahoma	71 Okla. Stat. Sec. 901 to 913
Oregon	Or. Rev. Stat. 59.535 to 59.585
Pennsylvania	20 Pa. Cons. Stat. 6401 to 6413
Rhode Island	R.I. Gen. Laws Sec. 7-11.1-1 to 7-11.1-12
South Carolina	S.C. Code Ann. Sec. 35-6-10 to 35-6-100
South Dakota	S.D. Codified Laws 29A-6-301 to 29A-6-311
Utah	Utah Code Ann. 1953, 75-6-301 to 75-6-313
Vermont	Vt. Stat. Ann., Secs. 4351 to 4360
Virginia	Va. Code Ann. 1950, Secs. 64.1-206.1 to 64.1-206.8

Washington	Wash. Rev. Code Sec. 21.35.005 to 21.35.901
West Virginia	W. Va. Code Secs. 36-10-1 to 36-10-12
Wisconsin	Wis. Stat. Ann. Sec. 705.21 to 705.30
Wyoming	Wyo. Stat. Ann.1977, Secs. 2-16-101 to 2-16-112

STATES IN WHICH A HANDWRITTEN LIST OF PERSONAL PROPERTY MAY BE USED WITH A WILL

In the following states a person may include a handwritten list with his or her will that lists items of personal property that are to go to specific persons. If the list is completely handwritten, dated before the date of the will, and signed in ink, it is legally binding. Next to the state is the statute citation.

NOTE: *In states that allow holographic (handwritten) wills (see page 84), you could also use a handwritten list of personal property.*

Alaska	Ala. Code Sec. 13.12.513
Arizona	Ariz. Rev. Stat. Sec. 14-2513
Arkansas	Ark. Stat. Ann. Sec. 28-25-107
Colorado	Colo. Rev. Stat. Ann. Sec. 15-11-513
Delaware	Del. Code Ann. Sec. 212
Florida	Fla. Stat. Sec. 732.515
Hawaii	Haw. Rev. Stat. Sec. 560: 2-513
Idaho	Idaho Code Sec. 15-2-513
Iowa	Iowa Code Sec. 633.276
Kansas	Kan. Stat. Ann. Sec. 59-623
Maine	Me. Rev. Stat. Ann.18A. Sec. 2-513
Michigan	Mich. Comp. Laws Ann. Sec. 700.2513
Minnesota	Minn. Stat. Ann. Sec. 524.2-513
Missouri	Mo. Rev. Stat. Sec. 474.333
Montana	Mont. Code Ann. Sec. 72-2-533
Nebraska	Neb. Rev. Stat. 1943, Sec. 30-2338
Nevada	Nev. Rev. Stat. Sec. 133.045
New Jersey	N.J. Rev. Stat. Sec. 3B:3-11

New Mexico	N.M. Stat. Ann. Sec. 45-2-513
North Dakota	N.D.Cent. Code Sec. 30.1-08-13
South Carolina	S.C. Code Ann. Sec. 62-2-512
South Dakota	S.D. Codified Laws. 29a-2-513
Utah	Utah Code Ann. 75-2-513
Virginia	Va. Code Ann. Sec. 64.1-45.1
Washington	Wash. Rev. Code Sec. 11.12.260
Wisconsin	Wis. Stat. Sec. 853.32
Wyoming	Wyo. Stat. Ann. Sec. 2-6-124

STATES IN WHICH A HANDWRITTEN WILL IS LEGAL WITHOUT WITNESSES

In the following states, a will that is completely handwritten, signed, and dated by the testator is valid even if it not witnessed. However, it must be completely handwritten, with the complete date, and the testator's signature.

Alaska	Alaska Stat. Sec. 13.12.502
Arizona	Ariz. Rev. Stat. Sec. 14-2503
Arkansas	Ark.Code Ann. Sec. 28-25-104
California	Cal. Prob. Code Sec. 6111
Colorado	Colo. Rev. Stat. Ann. Sec. 15-11-502
Hawaii	Haw. Rev. Stat. Sec. 560:2-502
Idaho	Idaho Code Sec. 15-2-503
Kentucky	Ky. Rev. Stat. Ann. Sec. 392.040
Louisiana	C.C. Sec. 1575
Maine	Me. Rev. Stat. Ann. Sec. 2-503
Michigan	Mich. Comp. Laws Ann. Sec. 700.2502
Mississippi	Miss. Code Ann. Sec. 91-5-1
Montana	Mont. Code Ann. Sec. 72-2-522
Nebraska	Neb. Rev. Stat. 1943 Sec. 30-2328
Nevada	Nev. Rev. Stat. Sec. 133.030, 133.090, 136.190
New Jersey	N.J. Stat. Ann. Tit. 3B, c.3, Sec. 3
North Carolina	N.C. Gen. Stat. Sec. 31-3.4
North Dakota	N.D. Cent. Code 30.1-08-02
Oklahoma	Okla. Stat. Sec. 84-54
Pennsylvania	20 Pa. Cons. Stat. 2502
Puerto Rico	LPRA 31-2111; 32-2241
South Dakota	S.D. Codified Laws 29A-2-502

Tennessee	Tenn. Code Ann. Sec. 32-1-105
Texas	Tex. Prob. Code Ann. Sec. 60
Utah	Utah Code Ann. Sec. 75-2-503
Virginia	Va. Code Ann. Sec. 64.1-16
West Virginia	W.Va. Code Sec. 41-1-83
Wyoming	Wyo. Stat. Ann. Sec. 2-6-113

Sample, Filled-in Forms

The following pages include sample filled-in forms for some of the forms in Appendix C. They are filled out in different ways for different situations. You should look at all of them to see how the different sections can be completed.

TABLE OF FORMS

These forms are included on the following pages:

NOTE: *The Ethical Will has no corresponding form in Appendix C. It must be written entirely by you.*

Simple Will—Spouse and Minor Children—One Guardian

Last Will and Testament

I, _____ John Smith _____ a resident of _____ Macon _____
County, _____ Illinois _____ do hereby make, publish, and declare this to be my
Last Will and Testament, hereby revoking any and all Wills and Codicils heretofore
made by me.

FIRST: I direct that all my just debts and funeral expenses be paid out of my estate as
soon after my death as is practicable.

SECOND: I give, devise, and bequeath the following specific gifts:
To my son, John A. Smith, my collection of rare coins; To my daughter Jane Smith,
the book collection my mother left me.

THIRD: I give, devise, and bequeath all my estate, real, personal, and mixed, of
whatever kind and wherever situated, of which I may die seized or possessed, or in
which I may have any interest or over which I may have any power of appointment or
testamentary disposition, to my spouse, _____ Barbara Smith _____.
If my said spouse does not survive me, I give, and bequeath the said property to my
children John A. Smith and Jane Smith in equal shares
_____, plus any
afterborn or adopted children in equal shares or their lineal descendants, per stirpes.

FOURTH: In the event that any beneficiary fails to survive me by thirty days, then this
will shall take effect as if that person had predeceased me.

FIFTH: Should my spouse not survive me, I hereby nominate, constitute, and appoint
_____ Larry Smith _____ as guardian over the person and
estate of any of my children who have not reached the age of majority at the time of my
death. In the event that said guardian is unable or unwilling to serve, then I nominate,
constitute, and appoint _____ Sally Rogers _____ as guardian.
Said guardian shall serve without bond or surety.

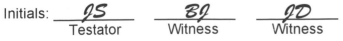

Initials: _*JS*_ _*BJ*_ _*JD*_ _____   Page _1_ of _2_
Testator   Witness   Witness   Witness

SIXTH: I hereby nominate, constitute, and appoint _____Barbara Smith_____
as Executor or Personal Representative of this, my Last Will and Testament. In the event that such named person is unable or unwilling to serve at any time or for any reason, then I nominate, constitute, and appoint _____Larry Smith_____
as Executor or Personal Representative in the place and stead of the person first named herein. It is my will and I direct that my Executor or Personal Representative shall not be required to furnish a bond for the faithful performance of his or her duties in any jurisdiction, any provision of law to the contrary notwithstanding, and I give my Executor or Personal Representative full power to administer my estate, including the power to settle claims, pay debts, and sell, lease or exchange real and personal property without court order.

IN WITNESS WHEREOF I declare this to be my Last Will and Testament and execute it willingly as my free and voluntary act for the purposes expressed herein and I am of legal age and sound mind and make this under no constraint or undue influence, this __29th_ day of _____August_____, 20_06_ at _____Decatur_____
State of _____Illinois_____.

_____*John Smith*_____

The foregoing instrument was on said date subscribed at the end thereof by _____John Smith_____, the above named Testator who signed, published, and declared this instrument to be his/her Last Will and Testament in the presence of us and each of us, who thereupon at his/her request, in his/her presence, and in the presence of each other, have hereunto subscribed our names as witnesses thereto. We are of sound mind and proper age to witness a will and understand this to be his/her will, and to the best of our knowledge testator is of legal age to make a will, of sound mind, and under no constraint or undue influence.

_____*Brenda Jones*_____ residing at _____Mara, Illinois_____

_____*John Doe*_____ residing at _____Decatur, Illinois_____

_____ residing at _____

Simple Will—Spouse and Minor Children—Two Guardians

Last Will and Testament

I, _____John Smith_____ a resident of ___New Hanover___ County, _____North Carolina_____ do hereby make, publish, and declare this to be my Last Will and Testament, hereby revoking any and all Wills and Codicils heretofore made by me.

FIRST: I direct that all my just debts and funeral expenses be paid out of my estate as soon after my death as is practicable.

SECOND: I give, devise, and bequeath the following specific gifts:
To my brother Larry, my collection of antique guns; To my sister Cathy, $1,000;
To my neighbor, Willie Lomax, my DeWalt power saw.

THIRD: I give, devise, and bequeath all my estate, real, personal, and mixed, of whatever kind and wherever situated, of which I may die seized or possessed, or in which I may have any interest or over which I may have any power of appointment or testamentary disposition, to my spouse, _____Barbara Smith_____.
If my said spouse does not survive me, I give, and bequeath the said property to my children _____John A. Smith and Brenda Smith_____, plus any afterborn or adopted children in equal shares or their lineal descendants, per stirpes.

FOURTH: In the event that any beneficiary fails to survive me by thirty days, then this will shall take effect as if that person had predeceased me.

FIFTH: Should my spouse not survive me, I hereby nominate, constitute, and appoint _____Larry Smith_____, as guardian over the person of any of my children who have not reached the age of majority at the time of my death. In the event that said guardian is unable or unwilling to serve, then I nominate, constitute, and appoint _____Sally Rogers_____ as guardian. Said guardian shall serve without bond or surety.

SIXTH: Should my spouse not survive me, I hereby nominate, constitute, and appoint _____ Sally Rogers _____ as guardian over the estate of any of my children who have not reached the age of majority at the time of my death. In the event that said guardian is unable or unwilling to serve, then I nominate, constitute, and appoint _____ Larry Smith _____ as guardian. Said guardian shall serve without bond or surety.

SEVENTH: I hereby nominate, constitute, and appoint _____ Larry Smith _____ as Executor or Personal Representative of this, my Last Will and Testament. In the event that such named person is unable or unwilling to serve at any time or for any reason, then I nominate, constitute, and appoint _____ Sally Rogers _____ as Executor or Personal Representative in the place and stead of the person first named herein. It is my will and I direct that my Executor or Personal Representative shall not be required to furnish a bond for the faithful performance of his or her duties in any jurisdiction, any provision of law to the contrary notwithstanding, and I give my Executor or Personal Representative full power to administer my estate, including the power to settle claims, pay debts, and sell, lease or exchange real and personal property without court order.

IN WITNESS WHEREOF I declare this to be my Last Will and Testament and execute it willingly as my free and voluntary act for the purposes expressed herein and I am of legal age and sound mind and make this under no constraint or undue influence, this _29th_ day of _____ August _____ , 20_06_ at _____ Wilmington _____ State of _____ North Carolina _____ .

_____ *John Smith* _____

The foregoing instrument was on said date subscribed at the end thereof by _____ John Smith _____ , the above named Testator who signed, published, and declared this instrument to be his/her Last Will and Testament in the presence of us and each of us, who thereupon at his/her request, in his/her presence, and in the presence of each other, have hereunto subscribed our names as witnesses thereto. We are of sound mind and proper age to witness a will and understand this to be his/her will, and to the best of our knowledge testator is of legal age to make a will, of sound mind, and under no constraint or undue influence.

_____ *Brenda Jones* _____ residing at _____ Wilmington, North Carolina _____

_____ *John Doe* _____ residing at _____ Wrightsville Beach, North Carolina _____

_____ residing at _____

Simple Will—Spouse and Minor Children—Guardian and Trust

Last Will and Testament

I, _____John Smith_____ a resident of ____Ingham____ County, _____Michigan_____ do hereby make, publish, and declare this to be my Last Will and Testament, hereby revoking any and all Wills and Codicils heretofore made by me.

FIRST: I direct that all my just debts and funeral expenses be paid out of my estate as soon after my death as is practicable.

SECOND: I give, devise, and bequeath the following specific gifts:
To my sister, Sally Rogers, our grandmother's china our mother left to me in her will.

THIRD: I give, devise, and bequeath all my estate, real, personal, and mixed, of whatever kind and wherever situated, of which I may die seized or possessed, or in which I may have any interest or over which I may have any power of appointment or testamentary disposition, to my spouse, _____Barbara Smith_____. If my said spouse does not survive me, I give, and bequeath the said property to my children __John A. Smith and Brenda Smith__ _____, plus any afterborn or adopted children in equal shares or their lineal descendants, per stirpes.

FOURTH: In the event that any beneficiary fails to survive me by thirty days, then this will shall take effect as if that person had predeceased me.

FIFTH: In the event that any of my children have not reached the age of ____21____ years at the time of my death, then the share of any such child shall be held in a separate trust by _____Larry Smith_____ for such child.

The trustee shall use the income and that part of the principal of the trust as is, in the trustee's sole discretion, necessary or desirable to provide proper housing, medical care, food, clothing, entertainment and education for the trust beneficiary, considering the beneficiary's other resources. Any income that is not distributed shall be added to the principal. Additionally, the trustee shall have all powers conferred by the law of the state having jurisdiction over this trust, as well as the power to pay from the assets of the trust reasonable fees necessary to administer the trust.

The trust shall terminate when the child reaches the age specified above and the remaining assets distributed to the child, unless they have been exhausted sooner. In the event the child dies prior to the termination of the trust, then the assets shall pass to the estate of the child. The interests of the beneficiary under this trust shall not be assignable and shall be free from the claims of creditors to the full extent allowed by law.

Initials: ___*JS*___ ___*BJ*___ ___*JD*___ _____   Page __1__ of __2__
　　　　　　Testator　　Witness　　Witness　　Witness

In the event the said trustee is unable or unwilling to serve for any reason, then I nominate, constitute, and appoint _____Sally Rogers_____ as alternate trustee. No bond shall be required of either trustee in any jurisdiction and this trust shall be administered without court supervision as allowed by law.

SIXTH: Should my spouse not survive me, I hereby nominate, constitute, and appoint _____Larry Smith_____ as guardian over the person and estate of any of my children who have not reached the age of majority at the time of my death. In the event that said guardian is unable or unwilling to serve, then I nominate, constitute, and appoint _____Sally Rogers_____ as guardian.

SEVENTH: I hereby nominate, constitute, and appoint _____Barbara Smith_____ as Executor or Personal Representative of this, my Last Will and Testament. In the event that such named person is unable or unwilling to serve at any time or for any reason, then I nominate, constitute, and appoint _____Larry Smith_____ as Executor or Personal Representative in the place and stead of the person first named herein. It is my will and I direct that my Executor or Personal Representative shall not be required to furnish a bond for the faithful performance of his or her duties in any jurisdiction, any provision of law to the contrary notwithstanding, and I give my Executor or Personal Representative full power to administer my estate, including the power to settle claims, pay debts, and sell, lease or exchange real and personal property without court order.

IN WITNESS WHEREOF I declare this to be my Last Will and Testament and execute it willingly as my free and voluntary act for the purposes expressed herein and I am of legal age and sound mind and make this under no constraint or undue influence, this __1st__ day of ___December___, 20_06_ at _____Lansing_____ State of _____Michigan_____.

_____*John Smith*_____

The foregoing instrument was on said date subscribed at the end thereof by _____John Smith_____, the above named Testator who signed, published, and declared this instrument to be his/her Last Will and Testament in the presence of us and each of us, who thereupon at his/her request, in his/her presence, and in the presence of each other, have hereunto subscribed our names as witnesses thereto. We are of sound mind and proper age to witness a will and understand this to be his/her will, and to the best of our knowledge testator is of legal age to make a will, of sound mind, and under no constraint or undue influence.

_____*Brenda Jones*_____ residing at _____Lansing, Michigan_____

_____*John Doe*_____ residing at _____Lansing, Michigan_____

_____ residing at _____

Simple Will—Spouse and No Children (Survivor)

Last Will and Testament

I, _____John Smith_____ a resident of _____Dade_____
County, _____Florida_____ do hereby make, publish, and declare this to be my
Last Will and Testament, hereby revoking any and all Wills and Codicils heretofore
made by me.

FIRST: I direct that all my just debts and funeral expenses be paid out of my estate as
soon after my death as is practicable.

SECOND: I give, devise, and bequeath the following specific gifts:
I may leave a statement or list disposing of certain items of my tangible personal
property. Any such statement or list in existence at the time of my death shall be
determinative with respect to all items bequeathed therein.

NOTE: *This clause is only legal in certain states, see Appendix A.*

THIRD: I give, devise, and bequeath all my estate, real, personal, and mixed, of
whatever kind and wherever situated, of which I may die seized or possessed, or in
which I may have any interest or over which I may have any power of appointment or
testamentary disposition, to my spouse, _____Barbara Smith_____.
If my said spouse does not survive me, I give, and bequeath the said property to
my sisters, Jan Smith, Joan Smith, and Jennifer Smith in equal shares
_____
_____, or the survivor of them.

FOURTH: In the event that any beneficiary fails to survive me by thirty days, then this
will shall take effect as if that person had predeceased me.

FIFTH: I hereby nominate, constitute, and appoint _____Barbara Smith_____
as Executor or Personal Representative of this, my Last Will and Testament. In the
event that such named person is unable or unwilling to serve at any time or for any
reason, then I nominate, constitute, and appoint _____Reginald Smith_____
as Executor or Personal Representative in the place and stead of the person first
named herein. It is my will and I direct that my Executor or Personal Representative

Initials: ___*JS*___ ___*BJ*___ ___*JD*___ _____ Page _1_ of _2_
      Testator   Witness   Witness   Witness

shall not be required to furnish a bond for the faithful performance of his or her duties in any jurisdiction, any provision of law to the contrary notwithstanding, and I give my Executor or Personal Representative full power to administer my estate, including the power to settle claims, pay debts, and sell, lease or exchange real and personal property without court order.

IN WITNESS WHEREOF I declare this to be my Last Will and Testament and execute it willingly as my free and voluntary act for the purposes expressed herein and I am of legal age and sound mind and make this under no constraint or undue influence, this __29th__ day of _____August_____, 20_06_ at _____Miami Beach_____ State of _____Florida_____.

_____*John Smith*_____

The foregoing instrument was on said date subscribed at the end thereof by _____John Smith_____, the above named Testator who signed, published, and declared this instrument to be his/her Last Will and Testament in the presence of us and each of us, who thereupon at his/her request, in his/her presence, and in the presence of each other, have hereunto subscribed our names as witnesses thereto. We are of sound mind and proper age to witness a will and understand this to be his/her will, and to the best of our knowledge testator is of legal age to make a will, of sound mind, and under no constraint or undue influence.

_____*Brenda Jones*_____ residing at _____West Palm Beach, Florida_____

_____*John Doe*_____ residing at _____Key Largo, Florida_____

_____ residing at _____

Simple Will—Spouse and No Children (Others or Their Descendants)

Last Will and Testament

I, _____John Smith_____ a resident of _____Marion_____
County, _____Indiana_____ do hereby make, publish, and declare this to be my
Last Will and Testament, hereby revoking any and all Wills and Codicils heretofore
made by me.

FIRST: I direct that all my just debts and funeral expenses be paid out of my estate as
soon after my death as is practicable.

SECOND: I give, devise, and bequeath the following specific gifts:
To my alma mater, State University, $10,000; To the Indianapolis Pet Shelter and
Care Center, $500.

THIRD: I give, devise, and bequeath all my estate, real, personal, and mixed, of
whatever kind and wherever situated, of which I may die seized or possessed, or in
which I may have any interest or over which I may have any power of appointment or
testamentary disposition, to my spouse, _____Barbara Smith_____.
If my said spouse does not survive me, I give, and bequeath the said property to
my brother, Larry Smith
_____
_____
_____, or to his lineal descendants, per stirpes.

FOURTH: In the event that any beneficiary fails to survive me by thirty days, then this
will shall take effect as if that person had predeceased me.

FIFTH: I hereby nominate, constitute, and appoint _____Barbara Smith_____
as Executor or Personal Representative of this, my Last Will and Testament. In the
event that such named person is unable or unwilling to serve at any time or for any
reason, then I nominate, constitute, and appoint _____Larry Smith_____
as Executor or Personal Representative in the place and stead of the person first
named herein. It is my will and I direct that my Executor or Personal Representative

Initials:  _JS_   _BJ_   _JD_   _____   Page _1_ of _2_
       Testator   Witness   Witness   Witness

shall not be required to furnish a bond for the faithful performance of his or her duties in any jurisdiction, any provision of law to the contrary notwithstanding, and I give my Executor or Personal Representative full power to administer my estate, including the power to settle claims, pay debts, and sell, lease or exchange real and personal property without court order.

IN WITNESS WHEREOF I declare this to be my Last Will and Testament and execute it willingly as my free and voluntary act for the purposes expressed herein and I am of legal age and sound mind and make this under no constraint or undue influence, this __1st__ day of _____December_____, 20_06_ at _____Indianapolis_____ State of _____Indiana_____.

_____*John Smith*_____

The foregoing instrument was on said date subscribed at the end thereof by _____John Smith_____, the above named Testator who signed, published, and declared this instrument to be his/her Last Will and Testament in the presence of us and each of us, who thereupon at his/her request, in his/her presence, and in the presence of each other, have hereunto subscribed our names as witnesses thereto. We are of sound mind and proper age to witness a will and understand this to be his/her will, and to the best of our knowledge testator is of legal age to make a will, of sound mind, and under no constraint or undue influence.

_____*Brenda Jones*_____ residing at _____Indianapolis, Indiana_____

_____*John Doe*_____ residing at _____Indianapolis, Indiana_____

_____ residing at _____

Simple Will—Spouse and Adult Children (All to Spouse)

Last Will and Testament

I, _____John Smith_____ a resident of _____Tioga_____ County, _____New York_____ do hereby make, publish, and declare this to be my Last Will and Testament, hereby revoking any and all Wills and Codicils heretofore made by me.

FIRST: I direct that all my just debts and funeral expenses be paid out of my estate as soon after my death as is practicable.

SECOND: I give, devise, and bequeath the following specific gifts:
 I leave my 1999 GT Celica to my daughter Beamy Smith. I leave my entire coin collection to my daughter Seamy Smith. I leave my Chris Craft boat and trailer to my
 daughter Amy. In the event my said daughters predecease me, said gifts shall be
 part of the residue of my estate.

THIRD: I give, devise, and bequeath all my estate, real, personal, and mixed, of whatever kind and wherever situated, of which I may die seized or possessed, or in which I may have any interest or over which I may have any power of appointment or testamentary disposition, to my spouse, _____Barbara Smith_____.
If my said spouse does not survive me, I give, and bequeath the said property to my children Amy Smith, Beamy Smith, and Seamy Smith

_____, in equal shares or to their lineal descendants, per stirpes.

FOURTH: In the event that any beneficiary fails to survive me by thirty days, then this will shall take effect as if that person had predeceased me.

FIFTH: I hereby nominate, constitute, and appoint _____Barbara Smith_____ as Executor or Personal Representative of this, my Last Will and Testament. In the event that such named person is unable or unwilling to serve at any time or for any reason, then I nominate, constitute, and appoint _____Reginald Smith_____ as Executor or Personal Representative in the place and stead of the person first named herein. It is my will and I direct that my Executor or Personal Representative

Initials: ___*JS*___ ___*BJ*___ ___*JD*___ _____   Page _1_ of _2_
         Testator   Witness   Witness   Witness

shall not be required to furnish a bond for the faithful performance of his or her duties in any jurisdiction, any provision of law to the contrary notwithstanding, and I give my Executor or Personal Representative full power to administer my estate, including the power to settle claims, pay debts, and sell, lease or exchange real and personal property without court order.

IN WITNESS WHEREOF I declare this to be my Last Will and Testament and execute it willingly as my free and voluntary act for the purposes expressed herein and I am of legal age and sound mind and make this under no constraint or undue influence, this __5th__ day of _____June_____, 20 _06_ at _____Oswego_____ State of _____New York_____.

_____*John Smith*_____

The foregoing instrument was on said date subscribed at the end thereof by _____*John Smith*_____, the above named Testator who signed, published, and declared this instrument to be his/her Last Will and Testament in the presence of us and each of us, who thereupon at his/her request, in his/her presence, and in the presence of each other, have hereunto subscribed our names as witnesses thereto. We are of sound mind and proper age to witness a will and understand this to be his/her will, and to the best of our knowledge testator is of legal age to make a will, of sound mind, and under no constraint or undue influence.

_____*Brenda Jones*_____ residing at _____Oswego, New York_____

_____*John Doe*_____ residing at _____Ithaca, New York_____

_____ residing at _____

Simple Will—Spouse and Adult Children (To Spouse and Children)

Last Will and Testament

I, _____ John Smith _____ a resident of _____ Trumbull _____ County, _____ Ohio _____ do hereby make, publish, and declare this to be my Last Will and Testament, hereby revoking any and all Wills and Codicils heretofore made by me.

FIRST: I direct that all my just debts and funeral expenses be paid out of my estate as soon after my death as is practicable.

SECOND: I give, devise, and bequeath the following specific gifts:

THIRD: I give, devise, and bequeath all my estate, real, personal, and mixed, of whatever kind and wherever situated, of which I may die seized or possessed, or in which I may have any interest or over which I may have any power of appointment or testamentary disposition, as follows:

__50__ % to my spouse, _____ Barbara Smith _____ and
__50__ % to my children, __John A. Smith and Brenda Smith__ _____

_____, in equal shares or to their lineal descendants per stirpes.

FOURTH: In the event that any beneficiary fails to survive me by thirty days, then this will shall take effect as if that person had predeceased me.

FIFTH: I hereby nominate, constitute, and appoint _____ Barbara Smith _____ as Executor or Personal Representative of this, my Last Will and Testament. In the event that such named person is unable or unwilling to serve at any time or for any reason, then I nominate, constitute, and appoint _____ Larry Smith _____ as Executor or Personal Representative in the place and stead of the person first named herein. It is my will and I direct that my Executor or Personal Representative

Initials: __*JS*__ __*BJ*__ __*JD*__ _____   Page _1_ of _2_
         Testator   Witness   Witness   Witness

shall not be required to furnish a bond for the faithful performance of his or her duties in any jurisdiction, any provision of law to the contrary notwithstanding, and I give my Executor or Personal Representative full power to administer my estate, including the power to settle claims, pay debts, and sell, lease or exchange real and personal property without court order.

IN WITNESS WHEREOF I declare this to be my Last Will and Testament and execute it willingly as my free and voluntary act for the purposes expressed herein and I am of legal age and sound mind and make this under no constraint or undue influence, this __28th__ day of _____July_____, 20_06_ at _____Warren_____ State of _____Ohio_____.

_____*John Smith*_____

The foregoing instrument was on said date subscribed at the end thereof by _____John Smith_____, the above named Testator who signed, published, and declared this instrument to be his/her Last Will and Testament in the presence of us and each of us, who thereupon at his/her request, in his/her presence, and in the presence of each other, have hereunto subscribed our names as witnesses thereto. We are of sound mind and proper age to witness a will and understand this to be his/her will, and to the best of our knowledge testator is of legal age to make a will, of sound mind, and under no constraint or undue influence.

_____*Brenda Jones*_____ residing at _____Warren, Ohio_____

_____*John Doe*_____ residing at _____Courtland, Ohio_____

_____ residing at _____

Simple Will—No Spouse—Minor Children—One Guardian

Last Will and Testament

I, _____ John Smith _____ a resident of _____ Clarion _____ County, _____ Pennsylvania _____ do hereby make, publish, and declare this to be my Last Will and Testament, hereby revoking any and all Wills and Codicils heretofore made by me.

FIRST: I direct that all my just debts and funeral expenses be paid out of my estate as soon after my death as is practicable.

SECOND: I give, devise, and bequeath the following specific gifts:
All of my household furnishings to my sister, Sally Rogers; All my home electronics to my brother, Larry Smith; My college football trophy to my son, John A. Smith; The wedding album of her mother and me to my daughter, Brenda Smith.

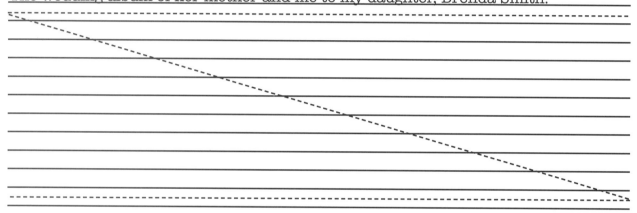

THIRD: I give, devise, and bequeath all my estate, real, personal, and mixed, of whatever kind and wherever situated, of which I may die seized or possessed, or in which I may have any interest or over which I may have any power of appointment or testamentary disposition, to my children _____ John A. Smith and Brenda Smith _____

_____, plus any afterborn or adopted children in equal shares or to their lineal descendants per stirpes.

FOURTH: In the event that any beneficiary fails to survive me by thirty days, then this will shall take effect as if that person had predeceased me.

FIFTH: In the event any of my children have not attained the age of 18 years at the time of my death, I hereby nominate, constitute, and appoint _____ Larry Smith _____ as guardian over the person and estate of any of my children who have not reached the age of majority at the time of my death. In the event that said guardian is unable or unwilling to serve, then I nominate, constitute, and appoint _____ Sally Rogers _____ as guardian. Said guardian shall serve without bond or surety.

Initials: ___ *JS* ___   ___ *BJ* ___   ___ *JD* ___   _____   Page _1_ of _2_
           Testator   Witness   Witness   Witness

SIXTH: I hereby nominate, constitute, and appoint _____ Larry Smith _____
as Executor or Personal Representative of this, my Last Will and Testament. In the event that such named person is unable or unwilling to serve at any time or for any reason, then I nominate, constitute, and appoint _____ Sally Rogers _____
as Executor or Personal Representative in the place and stead of the person first named herein. It is my will and I direct that my Executor or Personal Representative shall not be required to furnish a bond for the faithful performance of his or her duties in any jurisdiction, any provision of law to the contrary notwithstanding, and I give my Executor or Personal Representative full power to administer my estate, including the power to settle claims, pay debts, and sell, lease or exchange real and personal property without court order.

IN WITNESS WHEREOF I declare this to be my Last Will and Testament and execute it willingly as my free and voluntary act for the purposes expressed herein and I am of legal age and sound mind and make this under no constraint or undue influence, this __31st__ day of _____ October _____, 20_06_ at _____ Clarion _____
State of _____ Pennsylvania _____.

_____ *John Smith* _____

The foregoing instrument was on said date subscribed at the end thereof by _____ John Smith _____, the above named Testator who signed, published, and declared this instrument to be his/her Last Will and Testament in the presence of us and each of us, who thereupon at his/her request, in his/her presence, and in the presence of each other, have hereunto subscribed our names as witnesses thereto. We are of sound mind and proper age to witness a will and understand this to be his/her will, and to the best of our knowledge testator is of legal age to make a will, of sound mind, and under no constraint or undue influence.

_____ *Brenda Jones* _____ residing at _____ Clarion, Pennsylvania _____

_____ *John Doe* _____ residing at _____ Clarion, Pennsylvania _____

_____ residing at _____

Simple Will—No Spouse—Minor Children—Guardian Over Persons, Guardian Over Property

Last Will and Testament

I, _____ John Doe _____ a resident of _____ Fairfax _____
County, _____ Virginia _____ do hereby make, publish, and declare this to be my
Last Will and Testament, hereby revoking any and all Wills and Codicils heretofore
made by me.

FIRST: I direct that all my just debts and funeral expenses be paid out of my estate as
soon after my death as is practicable.

SECOND: I give, devise, and bequeath the following specific gifts:
___—NONE—_____

_____
_____
_____
_____
_____
_____
_____
_____
_____
_____
_____
_____
_____

THIRD: I give, devise, and bequeath all my estate, real, personal, and mixed, of
whatever kind and wherever situated, of which I may die seized or possessed, or in
which I may have any interest or over which I may have any power of appointment or
testamentary disposition, to my children _James Doe, Mary Doe, Larry Doe, Barry_____
_Doe, Carrie Doe, and Moe Doe._____

_____, plus any afterborn or adopted children in equal shares
or to their lineal descendants per stirpes.

FOURTH: In the event that any beneficiary fails to survive me by thirty days, then this
will shall take effect as if that person had predeceased me.

FIFTH: In the event any of my children have not attained the age of 18 years at the time
of my death, I hereby nominate, constitute, and appoint _____ Herbert Doe _____
as guardian over the person of any of my children who have not reached the age of
majority at the time of my death. In the event that said guardian is unable or unwilling to
serve, then I nominate, constitute, and appoint _____ Tom Doe _____
as guardian. Said guardian shall serve without bond or surety.

Initials: _____ _____ _____ _____   Page _1_ of _2_
       Testator   Witness   Witness   Witness

SIXTH: In the event any of my children have not attained the age of 18 years at the time of my death, I hereby nominate, constitute, and appoint _____Herbert Doe_____ as guardian over the estate of any of my children who have not reached the age of majority at the time of my death. In the event that said guardian is unable or unwilling to serve, then I nominate, constitute, and appoint _____Tom Doe_____ as guardian. Said guardian shall serve without bond or surety.

SEVENTH: I hereby nominate, constitute, and appoint _____Clarence Doe_____ as Executor or Personal Representative of this, my Last Will and Testament. In the event that such named person is unable or unwilling to serve at any time or for any reason, then I nominate, constitute, and appoint _____Englebert Doe_____ as Executor or Personal Representative in the place and stead of the person first named herein. It is my will and I direct that my Executor or Personal Representative shall not be required to furnish a bond for the faithful performance of his or her duties in any jurisdiction, any provision of law to the contrary notwithstanding, and I give my Executor or Personal Representative full power to administer my estate, including the power to settle claims, pay debts, and sell, lease or exchange real and personal property without court order.

IN WITNESS WHEREOF I declare this to be my Last Will and Testament and execute it willingly as my free and voluntary act for the purposes expressed herein and I am of legal age and sound mind and make this under no constraint or undue influence, this _10th_ day of _____July_____, 20_06_ at _____Fairfax_____ State of _____Virginia_____.

_____*John Doe*_____

The foregoing instrument was on said date subscribed at the end thereof by _____John Doe_____, the above named Testator who signed, published, and declared this instrument to be his/her Last Will and Testament in the presence of us and each of us, who thereupon at his/her request, in his/her presence, and in the presence of each other, have hereunto subscribed our names as witnesses thereto. We are of sound mind and proper age to witness a will and understand this to be his/her will, and to the best of our knowledge testator is of legal age to make a will, of sound mind, and under no constraint or undue influence.

_____*Jane Roe*_____ residing at _____Falls Church, Virginia_____

_____*Melvin Coe*_____ residing at _____Burke, Virginia_____

_____ residing at _____

Simple Will—No Spouse—Minor Children—Guardian and Trust

Last Will and Testament

I, _____John Smith_____ a resident of _____Middlesex_____ County, ___Massachusetts___ do hereby make, publish, and declare this to be my Last Will and Testament, hereby revoking any and all Wills and Codicils heretofore made by me.

FIRST: I direct that all my just debts and funeral expenses be paid out of my estate as soon after my death as is practicable.

SECOND: I give, devise, and bequeath the following specific gifts: My collection of Superman memorabilia to the Superman Museum in Metropolis, Illinois.

THIRD: I give, devise, and bequeath all my estate, real, personal, and mixed, of whatever kind and wherever situated, of which I may die seized or possessed, or in which I may have any interest or over which I may have any power of appointment or testamentary disposition, to my children _____John A. Smith and Brenda Smith_____ _____, plus any afterborn or adopted children in equal shares or to their lineal descendants per stirpes.

FOURTH: In the event that any beneficiary fails to survive me by thirty days, then this will shall take effect as if that person had predeceased me.

FIFTH: In the event that any of my children have not reached the age of ___18___ years at the time of my death, then the share of any such child shall be held in a separate trust by _____Larry Smith_____ for such child.

The trustee shall use the income and that part of the principal of the trust as is, in the trustee's sole discretion, necessary or desirable to provide proper housing, medical care, food, clothing, entertainment and education for the trust beneficiary, considering the beneficiary's other resources. Any income that is not distributed shall be added to the principal. Additionally, the trustee shall have all powers conferred by the law of the state having jurisdiction over this trust, as well as the power to pay from the assets of the trust reasonable fees necessary to administer the trust.

The trust shall terminate when the child reaches the age specified above and the remaining assets distributed to the child, unless they have been exhausted sooner. In the event the child dies prior to the termination of the trust, then the assets shall pass to the estate of the child. The interests of the beneficiary under this trust shall not be assignable and shall be free from the claims of creditors to the full extent allowed by law.

In the event the said trustee is unable or unwilling to serve for any reason, then I nominate, constitute, and appoint _____Sally Rogers_____as alternate trustee. No bond shall be required of either trustee in any jurisdiction and this trust shall be administered without court supervision as allowed by law.

SIXTH: In the event any of my children have not attained the age of 18 years at the time of my death, I hereby nominate, constitute, and appoint _____Larry Smith_____ as guardian over the person and estate of any of my children who have not reached the age of majority at the time of my death. In the event that said guardian is unable or unwilling to serve, then I nominate, constitute, and appoint _____Sally Rogers_____ as guardian. Said guardian shall serve without bond or surety.

SEVENTH: I hereby nominate, constitute, and appoint _____Larry Smith_____ as Executor or Personal Representative of this, my Last Will and Testament. In the event that such named person is unable or unwilling to serve at any time or for any reason, then I nominate, constitute, and appoint _____Sally Rogers_____ as Executor or Personal Representative in the place and stead of the person first named herein. It is my will and I direct that my Executor or Personal Representative shall not be required to furnish a bond for the faithful performance of his or her duties in any jurisdiction, any provision of law to the contrary notwithstanding, and I give my Executor or Personal Representative full power to administer my estate, including the power to settle claims, pay debts, and sell, lease or exchange real and personal property without court order.

IN WITNESS WHEREOF I declare this to be my Last Will and Testament and execute it willingly as my free and voluntary act for the purposes expressed herein and I am of legal age and sound mind and make this under no constraint or undue influence, this __28th__ day of _____September_____, 20_06_ at _____Newton_____ State of ____Massachusetts____.

_____ _John Smith_ _____

The foregoing instrument was on said date subscribed at the end thereof by _____John Smith_____, the above named Testator who signed, published, and declared this instrument to be his/her Last Will and Testament in the presence of us and each of us, who thereupon at his/her request, in his/her presence, and in the presence of each other, have hereunto subscribed our names as witnesses thereto. We are of sound mind and proper age to witness a will and understand this to be his/her will, and to the best of our knowledge testator is of legal age to make a will, of sound mind, and under no constraint or undue influence.

_____Brenda Jones_____ residing at _____Newton, Massachusetts_____

_____John Doe_____ residing at _____Newton, Massachusetts_____

_____ residing at _____

Simple Will—No Spouse—Adult Children (Equal by Family)

Last Will and Testament

I, _____ John Smith _____ a resident of _____ Benton _____ County, _____ Minnesota _____ do hereby make, publish, and declare this to be my Last Will and Testament, hereby revoking any and all Wills and Codicils heretofore made by me.

FIRST: I direct that all my just debts and funeral expenses be paid out of my estate as soon after my death as is practicable.

SECOND: I give, devise, and bequeath the following specific gifts:
<u>My car to my neighbor, Ethel Murray.</u>

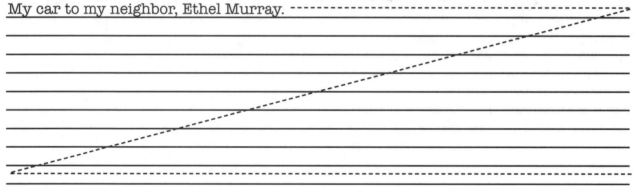

THIRD: I give, devise, and bequeath all my estate, real, personal, and mixed, of whatever kind and wherever situated, of which I may die seized or possessed, or in which I may have any interest or over which I may have any power of appointment or testamentary disposition, to my children _____ John A. Smith and Brenda Smith _____

_____, in equal shares, or their lineal descendants per stirpes.

FOURTH: In the event that any beneficiary fails to survive me by thirty days, then this will shall take effect as if that person had predeceased me.

FIFTH: I hereby nominate, constitute, and appoint _____ John A. Smith _____ as Executor or Personal Representative of this, my Last Will and Testament. In the event that such named person is unable or unwilling to serve at any time or for any reason, then I nominate, constitute, and appoint _____ Brenda Smith _____ as Executor or Personal Representative in the place and stead of the person first named herein. It is my will and I direct that my Executor or Personal Representative shall not be required to furnish a bond for the faithful performance of his or her duties in any jurisdiction, any provision of law to the contrary notwithstanding, and I give my Executor or Personal Representative full power to administer my estate, including the power to settle claims, pay debts, and sell, lease or exchange real and personal property without court order.

Initials: __*JS*__ __*BJ*__ __*JD*__ _____ Page _1_ of _2_
              Testator   Witness   Witness   Witness

IN WITNESS WHEREOF I declare this to be my Last Will and Testament and execute it willingly as my free and voluntary act for the purposes expressed herein and I am of legal age and sound mind and make this under no constraint or undue influence, this __15th__ day of _____November_____, 20_06_ at _____Rice_____ State of _____Minnesota_____ .

_____ *John Smith* _____

The foregoing instrument was on said date subscribed at the end thereof by _____John Smith_____, the above named Testator who signed, published, and declared this instrument to be his/her Last Will and Testament in the presence of us and each of us, who thereupon at his/her request, in his/her presence, and in the presence of each other, have hereunto subscribed our names as witnesses thereto. We are of sound mind and proper age to witness a will and understand this to be his/her will, and to the best of our knowledge testator is of legal age to make a will, of sound mind, and under no constraint or undue influence.

_____*Brenda Jones*_____ residing at _____Rice, Minnesota_____

_____*John Doe*_____ residing at _____Rice, Minnesota_____

_____ residing at _____

Simple Will—No Spouse—Adult Children (Equal by Person)

Last Will and Testament

I, _____ John Smith _____ a resident of ____ Los Angeles ____ County, _____ California _____ do hereby make, publish, and declare this to be my Last Will and Testament, hereby revoking any and all Wills and Codicils heretofore made by me.

FIRST: I direct that all my just debts and funeral expenses be paid out of my estate as soon after my death as is practicable.

SECOND: I give, devise, and bequeath the following specific gifts:
My mother's ruby ring to my granddaughter, Alexis Smith.

THIRD: I give, devise, and bequeath all my estate, real, personal, and mixed, of whatever kind and wherever situated, of which I may die seized or possessed, or in which I may have any interest or over which I may have any power of appointment or testamentary disposition, to my children _____ John A. Smith and Brenda Smith _____ _____, in equal shares, or their lineal descendants per capita.

FOURTH: In the event that any beneficiary fails to survive me by thirty days, then this will shall take effect as if that person had predeceased me.

FIFTH: I hereby nominate, constitute, and appoint _____ John A. Smith _____ as Executor or Personal Representative of this, my Last Will and Testament. In the event that such named person is unable or unwilling to serve at any time or for any reason, then I nominate, constitute, and appoint _____ Brenda Smith _____ as Executor or Personal Representative in the place and stead of the person first named herein. It is my will and I direct that my Executor or Personal Representative shall not be required to furnish a bond for the faithful performance of his or her duties in any jurisdiction, any provision of law to the contrary notwithstanding, and I give my Executor or Personal Representative full power to administer my estate, including the power to settle claims, pay debts, and sell, lease or exchange real and personal property without court order.

Initials: ___ *JS* ___ ___ *BJ* ___ ___ *JD* ___ _____   Page _1_ of _2_

Testator   Witness   Witness   Witness

IN WITNESS WHEREOF I declare this to be my Last Will and Testament and execute it willingly as my free and voluntary act for the purposes expressed herein and I am of legal age and sound mind and make this under no constraint or undue influence, this __3rd__ day of _____July_____, 20_06_ at _____Pomona_____ State of _____California_____ .

_____ _John Smith_ _____

The foregoing instrument was on said date subscribed at the end thereof by _____John Smith_____, the above named Testator who signed, published, and declared this instrument to be his/her Last Will and Testament in the presence of us and each of us, who thereupon at his/her request, in his/her presence, and in the presence of each other, have hereunto subscribed our names as witnesses thereto. We are of sound mind and proper age to witness a will and understand this to be his/her will, and to the best of our knowledge testator is of legal age to make a will, of sound mind, and under no constraint or undue influence.

_____Brenda Jones_____ residing at _____Pomona, California_____

_____John Doe_____ residing at _____Los Angeles, California_____

_____ residing at _____

Simple Will—No Spouse and No Children (To Survivor)

Last Will and Testament

I, _____John Smith_____ a resident of _____St. Louis_____ County, _____Missouri_____ do hereby make, publish, and declare this to be my Last Will and Testament, hereby revoking any and all Wills and Codicils heretofore made by me.

FIRST: I direct that all my just debts and funeral expenses be paid out of my estate as soon after my death as is practicable.

SECOND: I give, devise, and bequeath the following specific gifts:
My father's Medal of Honor to my nephew, Donald Smith.

THIRD: I give, devise, and bequeath all my estate, real, personal, and mixed, of whatever kind and wherever situated, of which I may die seized or possessed, or in which I may have any interest or over which I may have any power of appointment or testamentary disposition, to the following: _____Larry Smith and Sally Rogers_____ _____, in equal share, or to the survivor of them.

FOURTH: In the event that any beneficiary fails to survive me by thirty days, then this will shall take effect as if that person had predeceased me.

FIFTH: I hereby nominate, constitute, and appoint _____Larry Smith_____ as Executor or Personal Representative of this, my Last Will and Testament. In the event that such named person is unable or unwilling to serve at any time or for any reason, then I nominate, constitute, and appoint _____Sally Rogers_____ as Executor or Personal Representative in the place and stead of the person first named herein. It is my will and I direct that my Executor or Personal Representative shall not be required to furnish a bond for the faithful performance of his or her duties in any jurisdiction, any provision of law to the contrary notwithstanding, and I give my Executor or Personal Representative full power to administer my estate, including the power to settle claims, pay debts, and sell, lease or exchange real and personal property without court order.

Initials: __*JS*__ __*BJ*__ __*JD*__ _____   Page _1_ of _2_
       Testator   Witness   Witness   Witness

IN WITNESS WHEREOF I declare this to be my Last Will and Testament and execute it willingly as my free and voluntary act for the purposes expressed herein and I am of legal age and sound mind and make this under no constraint or undue influence, this __25th__ day of _____October_____, 20 _06_ at _____St. Louis_____ State of _____Missouri_____ .

_____*John Smith*_____

The foregoing instrument was on said date subscribed at the end thereof by _____John Smith_____, the above named Testator who signed, published, and declared this instrument to be his/her Last Will and Testament in the presence of us and each of us, who thereupon at his/her request, in his/her presence, and in the presence of each other, have hereunto subscribed our names as witnesses thereto. We are of sound mind and proper age to witness a will and understand this to be his/her will, and to the best of our knowledge testator is of legal age to make a will, of sound mind, and under no constraint or undue influence.

_____*Brenda Jones*_____ residing at _____St. Louis, Missouri_____

_____*John Doe*_____ residing at _____St. Louis, Missouri_____

_____ residing at _____

Simple Will—No Spouse and No Children (To Descendants)

Last Will and Testament

I, _____ John Smith _____ a resident of _____ Marion _____ County, _____ Oregon _____ do hereby make, publish, and declare this to be my Last Will and Testament, hereby revoking any and all Wills and Codicils heretofore made by me.

FIRST: I direct that all my just debts and funeral expenses be paid out of my estate as soon after my death as is practicable.

SECOND: I give, devise, and bequeath the following specific gifts:

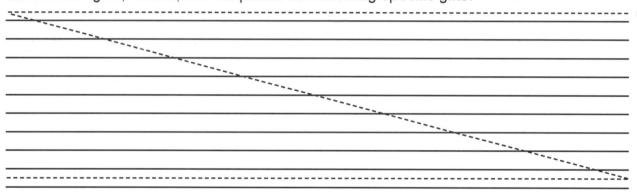

THIRD: I give, devise, and bequeath all my estate, real, personal, and mixed, of whatever kind and wherever situated, of which I may die seized or possessed, or in which I may have any interest or over which I may have any power of appointment or testamentary disposition, to the following: My brother Larry Smith and my sister Sally Rogers _____

_____, in equal shares, or their lineal descendants per stirpes.

FOURTH: In the event that any beneficiary fails to survive me by thirty days, then this will shall take effect as if that person had predeceased me.

FIFTH: I hereby nominate, constitute, and appoint _____ Larry Smith _____ as Executor or Personal Representative of this, my Last Will and Testament. In the event that such named person is unable or unwilling to serve at any time or for any reason, then I nominate, constitute, and appoint _____ Sally Rogers _____ as Executor or Personal Representative in the place and stead of the person first named herein. It is my will and I direct that my Executor or Personal Representative shall not be required to furnish a bond for the faithful performance of his or her duties in any jurisdiction, any provision of law to the contrary notwithstanding, and I give my Executor or Personal Representative full power to administer my estate, including the power to settle claims, pay debts, and sell, lease or exchange real and personal property without court order.

Initials: _JS_ _BJ_ _JD_ _____   Page _1_ of _2_
          Testator   Witness   Witness   Witness

IN WITNESS WHEREOF I declare this to be my Last Will and Testament and execute it willingly as my free and voluntary act for the purposes expressed herein and I am of legal age and sound mind and make this under no constraint or undue influence, this __2nd__ day of _____January_____, 20_07_ at _____Salem_____ State of _____Oregon_____ .

_____ _John Smith_ _____

The foregoing instrument was on said date subscribed at the end thereof by _____John Smith_____, the above named Testator who signed, published, and declared this instrument to be his/her Last Will and Testament in the presence of us and each of us, who thereupon at his/her request, in his/her presence, and in the presence of each other, have hereunto subscribed our names as witnesses thereto. We are of sound mind and proper age to witness a will and understand this to be his/her will, and to the best of our knowledge testator is of legal age to make a will, of sound mind, and under no constraint or undue influence.

_____Brenda Jones_____ residing at _____Salem, Oregon_____

_____John Doe_____ residing at _____West Salem, Oregon_____

_____ residing at _____

Self-Proved Will Affidavit
(attach to Will)

STATE OF _____ Illinois _____

COUNTY OF _____ Cook _____

We, _____ John Smith _____, and _____ Brenda Jones _____, and _____ John Doe _____, the testator and the witnesses, whose names are signed to the attached or foregoing instrument in those capacities, personally appearing before the undersigned authority and being first duly sworn, declare to the undersigned authority under penalty of perjury that: 1) the testator declared, signed, and executed the instrument as his or her last will; 2) he or she signed it willingly, or directed another to sign for him or her; 3) he or she executed it as his or her free and voluntary act for the purposes therein expressed; and 4) each of the witnesses, at the request of the testator, in his or her hearing and presence and in the presence of each other, signed the will as witnesses, and that to the best of his or her knowledge the testator was at that time of full legal age, of sound mind, and under no constraint or undue influence.

_____ *John Smith* _____ (Testator)

_____ *Brenda Jones* _____ (Witness)

_____ *John Doe* _____ (Witness)

Subscribed, sworn, and acknowledged before me _____ C.U. Sine _____, a notary public, and by _____ John Smith _____, the testator, and by _____ Brenda Jones _____ and _____ John Doe _____, witnesses, this __1st__ day of _____ December _____, 20 _06_ .

C.U. Sine _____
Notary public

Self-Proved Will Affidavit
(attach to Will)

STATE OF _____North Carolina_____

COUNTY OF _____Onslow_____

I, the undersigned, an officer authorized to administer oaths, certify that _____John Doe_____, the testator and _____Melvin Coe_____, and _____Jane Roe_____, the witnesses, whose names are signed to the attached or foregoing instrument and whose signatures appear below, having appeared before me and having been first been duly sworn, each then declared to me that: 1) the attached or foregoing instrument is the last will of the testator; 2) the testator willingly and voluntarily declared, signed, and executed the will in the presence of the witnesses; 3) the witnesses signed the will upon the request of the testator, in the presence and hearing of the testator and in the presence of each other; 4) to the best knowledge of each witness, the testator was, at the time of signing, of the age of majority (or otherwise legally competent to make a will), of sound mind and memory, and under no constraint or undue influence; and 5) each witness was and is competent and of proper age to witness a will.

_____*John Doe*_____ (Testator)

_____*Melvin Coe*_____ (Witness)

_____*Jane Roe*_____ (Witness)

Subscribed and sworn to before me by _____John Doe_____, the testator, who is personally known to me or who has produced _____*_____ as identification, and by _____Melvin Coe_____, a witness, who is personally known to me or who has produced _____*_____ as identification, and by _____Jane Roe_____, a witness, who is personally known to me or who has produced _____*_____ as identification, this _10th_ day of_____July_____, 20_06_.

C.U. Sine
Notary or other officer

> * **NOTE:** Identification is not required in every state

Notarial Will Page—Louisiana
(attach to Will)

STATE OF LOUISIANA

PARISH OF _____ Lincoln _____

The testator has signed this will at the end and on each other separate page, and has declared or signified in our presence that it is his or her last will and testament, and in the presence of the testator and each other we have hereunto subscribed our names this __30th__ day of ____November____, __2006__.

_____ *Albert Pickets* _____ (Testator)

_____ *Miranda Anderson* _____ (Witness)

_____ *Molly Wright* _____ (Witness)

On this __30th__ day of ____November____, __2006__ before me personally appeared _____ Albert Pickets _____, the testator, and ____ Miranda Anderson ____, and _____ Molly Wright _____, the witnesses, to me known to be the persons described in and who executed the foregoing instrument, and acknowledged that they executed it as their free act and deed.

Signed: _____ *C. U. Sine* _____
                              Notary

Note: In Louisiana a will must be signed on all pages by the testator. On page 1 replace "County" with "Parish."

Self-Proved Will Page—New Hampshire
(attach to Will)

The foregoing instrument was acknowledged before me this ___27th of October, 2006___
by _____John Smith_____ the testator; _____Brenda Jones_____
and _____John Doe_____, the witnesses, who under oath swear as
follows:

1. The testator signed the instrument as his will or expressly directed another to sign for him.

2. This was the testator's free and voluntary act for the purposes expressed in the will.

3. Each witness signed at the request of the testator, in his presence, and in the presence of the other witness.

4. To the best of my knowledge, at the time of the signing the testator was at least 18 years of age, or if under 18 years was a married person, and was of sane mind and under no constraint or undue influence.

C.U. Sine
Signature

Notary Public
Official Capacity

Initials: ___JS___   ___BJ___   ___JD___   _____   Page _1_ of _1_
      Testator   Witness   Witness   Witness

Self-Proved Will Affidavit—Texas
(attach to Will)

STATE OF TEXAS

COUNTY OF _____ Bexar _____

Before me, the undersigned authority, on this day personally appeared _John Smith_ _____, _____ Brenda Jones _____, and _____ John Doe _____, known to me to be the testator and the witnesses, respectively, whose names are subscribed to the annexed or foregoing instrument in their respective capacities, and, all of said persons being by me duly sworn, the said _____ John Smith _____ testator, declared to me and to the said witnesses in my presence that said instrument is his or her last will and testament, and that he or she had willingly made and executed it as his or her free act and deed, and the said witnesses, each on his or her oath stated to me in the presence and hearing of the said testator, that the said testator had declared to them that said instrument is his or her last will and testament, and that he or she executed same as such and wanted each of them to sign it as a witness; and upon their oaths each witness stated further that they did sign the same as witnesses in the presence of the said testator and at his or her request; that he or she was at the time eighteen years of age or over (or being under such age, was or had been lawfully married, or was then a member of the armed forces of the United States or an auxiliary thereof or of the Maritime Service) and was of sound mind; and that each of said witnesses was then at least fourteen years of age.

_____ *John Smith* _____ (Testator)

_____ *Brenda Jones* _____ (Witness)

_____ *John Doe* _____ (Witness)

Subscribed and sworn to before me by _____ John Smith _____, the testator, and by _____ Brenda Jones _____, and _____ John Doe _____, the witnesses, this _29th_ day of _September_, 20 _06_.

Signed: *C.U. Sine* _____

Notary Public _____
Official Capacity of Officer

First Codicil to the Will of

_____ Larry Lowe _____

I, _____ Larry Lowe _____, a resident of _____ Broome _____ County, _____ New York _____ declare this to be the first codicil to my Last Will and Testament dated _____ July 10 _____, _2006_.

FIRST: I hereby revoke the clause of my Will which reads as follows: FOURTH: I hereby leave $5000.00 to my daughter Mildred - .-

SECOND: I hereby add the following clause to my Will: FOURTH: I hereby leave $1000.000 to my daughter Mildred - .

THIRD: In all other respects I hereby confirm and republish my Last Will and Testament dated _____ July 10 _____, _2006_ .

IN WITNESS WHEREOF, I have signed, published, and declared the foregoing instrument as and for a codicil to my Last Will and Testament, this __3rd__ day of _____ January _____, 20_07_ .

_____ _Larry Lowe_ _____

The foregoing instrument was on the __3rd__ day of _____ January _____, _2007_, signed at the end thereof, and at the same time published and declared by _____ Larry Lowe _____, as and for a codicil to his/~~her~~ Last Will and Testament, dated _____ July 10 _____, 20_06_, in the presence of each of us, who, this attestation clause having been read to us, did at the request of the said testator/~~testatrix~~, in his/~~her~~ presence and in the presence of each other signed our names as witnesses thereto.

_____ _James Smith_ _____ residing at _____ Binghamton, New York _____

_____ _Mary Smith_ _____ residing at _____ Elmira, New York _____

_____ residing at _____

Self-Proved Codicil Affidavit
(attach to Codicil)

STATE OF _____ Oregon _____

COUNTY OF _____ Polk _____

We, _____ John Smith _____ and _____ Brenda Jones _____
and _____ John Doe _____, the testator and the witnesses, whose
names are signed to the attached or foregoing instrument in those capacities,
personally appearing before the undersigned authority and being first duly sworn,
declare to the undersigned authority under penalty of perjury that: 1) the testator
declared, signed, and executed the instrument as a codicil to his or her last will; 2) he or
she signed it willingly, or directed another to sign for him or her; 3) he or she executed it
as his or her free and voluntary act for the purposes therein expressed; and 4) each of
the witnesses, at the request of the testator, in his or her hearing and presence and in
the presence of each other, signed the will as witnesses, and that to the best of his or
her knowledge the testator was at that time of full legal age, of sound mind, and under
no constraint or undue influence.

_____ *John Smith* _____ (Testator)

_____ *Brenda Jones* _____ (Witness)

_____ *John Doe* _____ (Witness)

Subscribed, sworn, and acknowledged before me _____ C.U. Sine _____
a notary public, and by _____ John Smith _____, the testator, and
by _____ Brenda Jones _____ and _____ John Doe _____,
witnesses, this __1st__ day of _____ December _____, 20 _06_.

C.U. Sine _____
Notary public

Self-Proved Codicil Affidavit
(attach to Codicil)

STATE OF _____<u>Missouri</u>_____

COUNTY OF _____<u>St. Louis</u>_____

I, the undersigned, an officer authorized to administer oaths, certify that <u>John Smith</u> _____, the testator and _____<u>Brenda Jones</u>_____ and _____<u>John Doe</u>_____, the witnesses, whose names are signed to the attached or foregoing instrument and whose signatures appear below, having appeared before me and having first been duly sworn, each then declared to me that: 1) the attached or foregoing instrument is a codicil to the last will of the testator; 2) the testator willingly and voluntarily declared, signed, and executed the will in the presence of the witnesses; 3) the witnesses signed the will upon the request of the testator, in the presence and hearing of the testator and in the presence of each other; 4) to the best knowledge of each witness, the testator was, at the time of signing, of the age of majority (or otherwise legally competent to make a will), of sound mind and memory, and under no constraint or undue influence; and 5) each witness was and is competent and of proper age to witness a codicil to a will.

_____*John Smith*_____ (Testator)

_____*Brenda Jones*_____ (Witness)

_____*John Doe*_____ (Witness)

Subscribed and sworn to before me by _____<u>John Smith</u>_____, the testator, who is personally known to me or who has produced _____<u>a valid driver's license</u>_____ as identification, and by _____<u>Brenda Jones</u>_____ a witness who is personally known to me or who has produced _____<u>a valid driver's license</u>_____ as identification, and by _____<u>John Doe</u>_____, a witness, who is personally known to me or who has produced _____<u>a valid U.S. passport</u>_____ as identification, this __<u>8th</u>__ day of _____<u>February</u>_____, 20<u>07</u>.

C.U. Sine
_____
Notary or other officer

Self-Proved Codicil Affidavit
(attach to Codicil)

STATE OF TEXAS

COUNTY OF _____ Bexar _____

Before me, the undersigned authority, on this day personally appeared John Smith _____ , _____ Brenda Jones _____ , and _____ John Doe _____ , known to me to be the testator and the witnesses, respectively, whose names are subscribed to the annexed or foregoing instrument in their respective capacities, and, all of said persons being by me duly sworn, the said _____ John Smith _____ testator, declared to me and to the said witnesses in my presence that said instrument is his or her codicil, and that he or she had willingly made and executed it as his or her free act and deed, and the said witnesses, each on his or her oath stated to me in the presence and hearing of the said testator, that the said testator had declared to them that said instrument is his or her codicil, and that he or she executed same as such and wanted each of them to sign it as a witness; and upon their oaths each witness stated further that they did sign the same as witnesses in the presence of the said testator and at his or her request; that he or she was at the time eighteen years of age or over (or being under such age, was or had been lawfully married, or was then a member of the armed forces of the United States or an auxiliary thereof or of the Maritime Service) and was of sound mind; and that each of said witnesses was then at least fourteen years of age.

_____ *John Smith* _____ (Testator)

_____ *Brenda Jones* _____ (Witness)

_____ *John Doe* _____ (Witness)

Subscribed and sworn to before me by _____ John Smith _____ , the testator, and by _____ Brenda Jones _____ , and _____ John Doe _____ , the witnesses, this __8th__ day of _____ March _____ , 20 _07_ .

Signed: *C.U. Sine* _____

Notary Public _____
Official Capacity of Officer

Living Will

I, _____Sally Rogers_____, ____12/8/60____ (d/o/b) being of sound mind willfully and voluntarily make known my desires regarding my medical care and treatment under the circumstances as indicated below:

___SR___   1. If I should have an incurable or irreversible condition that will cause my death within a relatively short time, and if I am unable to make decisions regarding my medical treatment, I direct my attending physician to withhold or withdraw procedures that merely prolong the dying process and are not necessary to my comfort or to alleviate pain. This authorization includes, but is not limited to, the withholding or the withdrawal of the following types of medical treatment (subject to any special instructions in paragraph 5 below):

___✔___   a. Artificial feeding and hydration.
___✔___   b. Cardiopulmonary resuscitation (this includes, but is not limited to, the use of drugs, electric shock, and artificial breathing).
___✔___   c. Kidney dialysis.
___✔___   d. Surgery or other invasive procedures.
___✔___   e. Drugs and antibiotics.
___✔___   f. Transfusions of blood or blood products.
_____   g. Other: _____

_____

___SR___   2. If I should be in an irreversible coma or persistent vegetative state that my attending physician reasonably believes to be irreversible or incurable, I direct my attending physician to withhold or withdraw medical procedures and treatment other than such medical procedures and treatment necessary to my comfort or to alleviate pain. This authorization includes, but is not limited to, the withholding or withdrawal of the following types of medical treatment (subject to any special instructions in paragraph 5 below):

___✔___   a. Artificial feeding and hydration.
___✔___   b. Cardiopulmonary resuscitation (this includes, but is not limited to, the use of drugs, electric shock, and artificial breathing).
___✔___   c. Kidney dialysis.
___✔___   d. Surgery or other invasive procedures.
___✔___   e. Drugs and antibiotics.
___✔___   f. Transfusions of blood or blood products.
_____   g. Other: _____

_____

___SR___   3.   If I have a medical condition where I am unable to communicate my desires as to treatment and my physician determines that the burdens of treatment outweigh the expected benefits, I direct my attending physician to withhold or withdraw medical procedures and treatment other than such medical procedures and treatment necessary to my comfort or to alleviate pain. This authorization includes, but is not limited to, the withholding or withdrawal of the following types of medical treatment (subject to any special instructions in paragraph 5 below):

    ✔   a. Artificial feeding and hydration.

    ✔   b. Cardiopulmonary resuscitation (this includes, but is not limited to, the use of drugs, electric shock, and artificial breathing).

    ✔   c. Kidney dialysis.

    ✔   d. Surgery or other invasive procedures.

    ✔   e. Drugs and antibiotics.

    ✔   f. Transfusions of blood or blood products.

        g. Other: _____

_____

_____ 4. I want my life prolonged to the greatest extent possible (subject to any special instructions in paragraph 5 below).

_SR_ 5. Special instructions (if any) _NONE_____

_____

_____

_____

Signed this _20th_ day of _____December_____, 200_6_.

_Sally Rogers_____
Signature

Address: _123 Oak Street_____
_Atlanta, Georgia_____

The declarant is personally known to me and voluntarily signed this document in my presence.

Witness: _____*Brenda Jones*_____   Witness _____*John Doe*_____
Name: _____BRENDA JONES_____   Name: _____JOHN DOE_____
Address: _456 Maple Drive, Atlanta, Georgia_   Address: _342 Sycamore Drive, Atlanta, Georgia_

State of _____Georgia_____)
County of _____Fulton_____)

On this __20th__ day of _____December_____, 200__6__, before me, personally appeared _____Sally Rogers_____, principal, and _____Brenda Jones_____ and _____John Doe_____, witnesses, who are personally known to me or who provided _____driver's licenses_____ as identification, and signed the foregoing instrument in my presence.

_C.U. Sine_____
Notary Public

General Power of Attorney

_____ John Smith _____ (the Grantor)
hereby grants to _____ Barbara Smith _____
(the Agent) a general power of attorney. As the Grantor's attorney in fact, the Agent shall have full power and authority to undertake any and all acts, which may be lawfully undertaken on behalf of the grantor, including but not limited to: the right to buy, sell, lease, mortgage, assign, rent, or otherwise dispose of any real or personal property belonging to the Grantor; to execute, accept, undertake, and perform contracts in the name of the Grantor; to deposit, endorse, or withdraw funds to or from any bank depository of the Grantor; to initiate, defend, or settle legal actions on behalf of the Grantor; and to retain any accountant, attorney or other advisor deemed by the Agent to be necessary to protect the interests of the Grantor in relation to such powers.

By accepting this grant, the Agent agrees to act in a fiduciary capacity consistent with the reasonable best interests of the Grantor. This power of attorney may be revoked by the Grantor at any time; however, any person dealing with the Agent as attorney in fact may rely on this appointment until receipt of actual notice of termination.

IN WITNESS WHEREOF, the undersigned grantor has executed this power of attorney under seal as of the date stated above.

_John Smith_____(Seal)
Grantor

STATE OF
COUNTY OF

I certify that _____ John Smith _____, who
☑ is personally known to me to be the person whose name is subscribed to the foregoing instrument ☐ produced _____ as identification, personally appeared before me on _____October 30_____, 20__06__, and acknowledged the execution of the foregoing instrument.

_C.U. Sine_____
Notary Public, State of
Notary's commission expires:

I hereby accept the foregoing appointment as attorney in fact on _____October 30_____,
20_06_.

_Barbara Smith_____
Attorney in Fact

Specific Power of Attorney

_____John Smith_____ (the Grantor) hereby
grants to _____Barbara Smith_____ (the Agent)
a limited power of attorney. As the Grantor's attorney in fact, the Agent shall have full
power and authority to undertake and perform the following on behalf of the Grantor:

any and all action required in the sale of 123 Oak Street, Flora, Illinois.

By accepting this grant, the Agent agrees to act in a fiduciary capacity consistent with
the reasonable best interests of the Grantor. This power of attorney may be revoked by
the Grantor at any time; however, any person dealing with the Agent as attorney in fact
may rely on this appointment until receipt of actual notice of termination.

IN WITNESS WHEREOF, the undersigned grantor has executed this power of attorney
under seal as of the date stated above.

_John Smith_____(Seal)
Grantor

STATE OF
COUNTY OF

I certify that _____John Smith_____, who
☑ is personally known to me to be the person whose name is subscribed to the
foregoing instrument ☐ produced _____ as
identification, personally appeared before me on _____June 1_____, 20_07_,
and acknowledged the execution of the foregoing instrument.

_C.U. Sine_____
Notary Public, State of
Notary's commission expires:

I hereby accept the foregoing appointment as attorney in fact on _____June 1_____,
20_07_.

_Barbara Smith_____
Attorney in Fact

Revocation of Power of Attorney

I, _____John Smith_____ (the Grantor) granted a Power of Attorney to _____Barbara Smith_____ (the Agent) dated _____June 1, 2007_____, do hereby revoke said Power of Attorney as of _____June 19_____, 20_07_.

STATE OF
COUNTY OF

I certify that _____John Smith_____, who ☑ is personally known to me to be the person whose name is subscribed to the foregoing instrument ☐ produced _____ as identification, personally appeared before me on _____June 1_____, 20_07_, and acknowledged the execution of the foregoing instrument.

_C. U. Sine_____
Notary Public, State of
Notary's commission expires:

Health Care Power of Attorney

I, _____ Sally Rogers _____,
as principal, designate _____ Larry Smith _____
as my agent for all matters relating to my health care, including, without limitation, full power to give or refuse consent to all medical, surgical, hospital, and related health care. This power of attorney is effective on my inability to make or communicate health care decisions. All of my agent's actions under this power during any period when I am unable to make or communicate health care decisions or when there is uncertainty whether I am dead or alive have the same effect on my heirs, devisees, and personal representatives as if I were alive, competent, and acting for myself.

If my agent is unwilling or unable to serve or continue to serve, I hereby appoint
_____ John Smith _____ as my agent.

☑ I have   ☐ I have not completed and attached a living will for purposes of providing specific direction to my agent in situations that may occur during any period when I am unable to make or communicate health care decisions or after my death. My agent is directed to implement those choices I have initialed in the living will.
This health care directive continues in effect for all who may rely on it except those to whom I have given notice of its revocation.

Brenda Jones   _Brenda Jones_
Witness   Signature of Principal

42 West Drive, Indianapolis, Indiana   12/8/06
Address   Date

John Doe   1:00 p.m.
Witness   Time

439 Main Street, Indianapolis, Indiana 341 Maple Drive, Indianapolis, Indiana
Address   Address of Agent

                                        317-555-1212
                                        Telephone of Agent

Living Trust

THE
___John Smith___
REVOCABLE LIVING TRUST

I, _____John Smith_____, of _____Sarasota_____
_____Florida_____, hereby make and declare this Living Trust, as Grantor and Trustee, on ___January 2___, 20_07_.

This Trust shall be known as the _____John Smith_____ Revocable Living Trust. I, _____John Smith_____, will be trustee of this trust. Upon my death or if I am unable to manage this trust and my financial affairs, I appoint _____Larry Smith_____, my _____brother_____, of _____Sarasota, Florida_____ _____ as successor trustee, to serve without bond. In addition to any powers, authority, and discretion granted by law, I grant such Trustee and Successor Trustee any and all powers to perform any acts, in his or her sole discretion and without court approval, for the management and distribution of this trust.

TRANSFER OF PROPERTY. I hereby transfer to this trust the property listed on the attached Schedule of Assets which is made a part of this trust. I shall have the right at any time to add property to the trust or delete property from the trust.

DISPOSITION OF INCOME AND PRINCIPAL. During my lifetime, the Trustee shall pay so much or all of the net income and principal of the trust as I from time to time may request to me. Upon my death, the successor trustee shall pay all claims, expenses and taxes and shall distribute the trust estate to the following beneficiary or beneficiaries who shall survive me:
_my son, John A. Smith_____

The share of a beneficiary who is under _21_ years of age shall not be paid to such beneficiary but shall be held in trust by the Trustee. The Trustee shall pay so much or all of the net income and principal of such trust to the beneficiary as he thinks necessary for his or her support, welfare, and education. The Trustee shall pay the beneficiary the remaining principal, if any, when he or she attains the age of _25_ years.

In case a beneficiary for whom a share is held in trust dies before receiving the remaining principal, it shall be paid to his or her living child or children, or if none, to my then living descendants.

This trust shall terminate twenty-one (21) years after the death of the last beneficiary named in the trust.

REVOCATION AND AMENDMENT. I may, by signed instrument delivered to the Trustee, revoke or amend this Trust Agreement in whole or in part.

GOVERNING LAW. This Trust will be governed under the laws of the State of _____Florida_____.

In Witness Whereof, I as Grantor and Trustee, have executed this Agreement on the date above written.

_Brenda Jones_____   _John Smith_____
Witness   Grantor

_John Doe_____   _John Smith_____
Witness   Trustee

STATE OF   Florida   )
COUNTY OF Sarasota   )

The foregoing instrument was acknowledged before me this ___2nd___ day of _____January_____, 20_07_, by _____John Smith_____, as Grantor and Trustee, who is personally known to me or who has produced _____a valid driver's license_____ as identification.

_C.U. Sine_____
Notary Public
My Commission Expires:

ETHICAL WILL

To my children:

If you are reading this letter, then I have passed from this life. Don't cry for me, children, I have had a good life, probably better than most people who have ever lived before me. In my lifetime mankind has achieved so many miracles, from penicillin and laser surgery to putting a man on the moon and letting me fly across the ocean in a few hours to visit our relatives. I hope that you children see just as many wonders achieved in the rest of your lifetime.

You children are the greatest achievement of my life and I am proud of both of your accomplishments. I hope both of you will have children of your own so you experience what I experienced with you.

Meeting your mother was the most important event of my life and I feel like the luckiest man on earth to have had someone like her to have shared my life with. We had hard times, and disagreed sometimes like all couples, but we had each other and that was all that mattered.

Andy, I guess you understand that I left all the family photos to Margie because you never had an interest in them and she has been working on the family history. Margie, if Andy or his children ever show and interest in them, I ask you to make him copies of them.

Margie, I know you'll understand that I left Andy my antique guns.

In my life I have learned a few lessons I'd like to share with you. I hope that they make your lives a little easier:

- Don't always take life so seriously. Remember our old neighbor, Mr. Calabash, who never smiled? Think of how much better his life would have been if he had just lighten up and had a good time once in a while.

- Remember you will be as happy as you decide to be. There are people with cancer or who are blind who are as cheerful as can be and there are people without problems who are always miserable. It's up to you to decide if you will enjoy your glass because it is half full or complain and be miserable because it is half empty.

- Happiness is not a destination you can get to, it is the journey itself. If you think you'll be happy when you get a new car or a new house or a new spouse, you'll be disappointed when you get them. Happiness is always having new goals and getting closer to them each day.

- Know who you are. Take advantage of your talents and don't be afraid to try something new, but don't waste time on things you know you aren't good at.

In summary, children, I want to thank you for giving my life meaning and wish you the best of luck in all your endeavors.

Your loving father,

Joseph

Forms

The following pages contain forms that can be used to prepare a will, codicil, living will, and **UNIFORM DONOR CARD**. They should only be used by persons who have read this book, who do not have any complications in their legal affairs and who understand the forms they are using. The forms may be used right out of the book or they may be photocopied or retyped.

FORM 4: SIMPLE WILL—SPOUSE AND MINOR CHILDREN—
Use this will if you have minor children and want all your property to go to your spouse, but if your spouse dies previously, then to your minor children. It provides for two guardians, one over your children and one over their estates.

FORM 5: SIMPLE WILL—SPOUSE AND MINOR CHILDREN—
This will should be used if you have minor children and want all your property to go to your spouse, but if your spouse dies previously, then to your minor children. It provides for one person to be guardian over your children and for either the same person or another to be trustee over their property. This will allows your children's property to be held until they are older than 18 rather than distributing it all to them at age 18.

*Use this will if you want your property to go to your spouse but if your spouse predeceases you, to others or the **survivor** of the others.*

FORM 7: SIMPLE WILL—SPOUSE AND NO CHILDREN
*Use this will if you want your property to go to your spouse but if your spouse predeceases you, to others or the **descendants** of the others.*

FORM 8: SIMPLE WILL—SPOUSE AND ADULT CHILDREN
Use this will if you want all of your property to go to your spouse, but if your spouse dies previously, then to your children, all of whom are adults.

FORM 9: SIMPLE WILL—SPOUSE AND ADULT CHILDREN
Use this will if you want some of your property to go to your spouse, and some of your property to your children, all of whom are adults.

FORM 10: SIMPLE WILL—NO SPOUSE—MINOR CHILDREN—
Use this will if you do not have a spouse and want all your property to go to your children, at least one of whom is a minor. It provides for one person to be guardian over your children and their estates.

HOW TO PICK THE RIGHT WILL

Follow the chart and use the form number in the black circle, then use the affidavit in the black box.

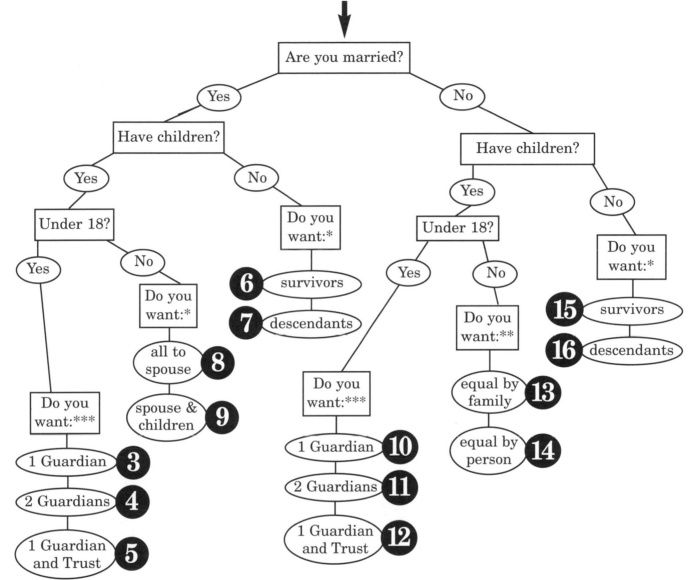

Use the **SELF-PROVED WILL AFFIDAVIT** for your state:

17 Alabama, Alaska, Arizona, Arkansas, Colorado, Connecticut, Hawaii, Idaho, Illinois, Indiana, Maine, Minnesota, Mississippi, Montana, Nebraska, Nevada, New Mexico, New York, North Dakota, Oregon, South Carolina, South Dakota, Tennessee, Utah, Washington, West Virginia.

18 Delaware, Georgia, Iowa, Kansas, Kentucky, Massachusetts, Missouri, New Jersey, North Carolina, Oklahoma, Pennsylvania, Rhode Island, Virginia, Wyoming.

19 Louisiana

20 New Hampshire

21 Texas

> *   For an explanation of survivors/descendants, see page 29.
> **   For an explanation of families/persons, see page 29.
> *** For an explanation of children's guardians and trust, see pages 31–32.

Asset and Beneficiary List

Property Inventory

Assets

Bank Accounts (checking, savings, certificates of deposit)

_____
_____
_____
_____
_____
_____
_____
_____

Real Estate

_____
_____
_____
_____
_____
_____
_____
_____

Vehicles (cars, trucks, boats, planes, RVs, etc.)

_____
_____
_____
_____
_____
_____
_____
_____
_____

Personal Property (collections, jewelry, tools, artwork, household items, etc.)

_____
_____
_____
_____
_____
_____
_____
_____

_____

_____

_____

_____

_____

_____

_____

_____

_____

_____

_____

_____

Stocks/Bonds/Mutual Funds

_____

_____

_____

_____

_____

_____

_____

_____

_____

_____

_____

_____

_____

_____

_____

_____

_____

_____

Retirement Accounts (IRAs, 401(k)s, pension plans, etc.)

_____

_____

_____

_____

_____

_____

_____

_____

_____

Receivables (mortgages held, notes, accounts receivable, personal loans)

_____
_____
_____
_____
_____
_____
_____
_____
_____

Life Insurance

_____
_____
_____
_____
_____
_____
_____
_____
_____

Other Property (trusts, partnerships, businesses, profit sharing, copyrights, etc.)

_____
_____
_____
_____
_____
_____
_____
_____
_____

Liabilities

Real Estate Loans

_____
_____
_____
_____
_____
_____
_____
_____

Vehicle Loans

_____
_____
_____
_____
_____
_____
_____
_____

Other Secured Loans

_____
_____
_____
_____
_____
_____
_____
_____
_____
_____

Unsecured Loans and Debts (taxes, child support, judgments, etc.)

_____
_____
_____
_____
_____
_____
_____
_____
_____
_____

Beneficiary List

Name	Address	Phone

Preferences and Information List
Statement of Desires and Location of Property and Documents

I, _____, am signing this document as the expression of my desires as to the matters stated below, and to inform my family members or other significant persons of the location of certain property and documents in the event of any emergency or of my death.

1. **Funeral Desires.** It is my desire that the following arrangements be made for my funeral and disposition of remains in the event of my death (state if you have made any arrangements, such as pre-paid burial plans, cemetery plots owned, etc.):

☐ Burial at _____
_____.

☐ Cremation at _____
_____.

☐ Other specific desires: _____
_____
_____.

2. **Pets.** I have the following pet(s): _____
_____. The following are my desires concerning the care of said pet(s): _____
_____

3. **Notification.** I would like the following person(s) notified in the event of emergency or death (give name, address and phone number):
_____
_____
_____
_____
_____.

4. **Location of Documents.** The following is a list of important documents, and their location:

☐ Last Will and Testament, dated _____. Location: _____
_____.

☐ Durable Power of Attorney, dated _____. Location: _____
_____.

☐ Living Will, dated _____. Location: _____
_____.

☐ Deed(s) to real estate (describe property location and location of deed):
_____
_____
_____

☐ Title(s) to vehicles (cars, boats, etc.) (Describe vehicle, its location, and location of title, registration, or other documents):

_____
_____
_____

☐ Life insurance policies (list name, address, and phone number of insurance company and insurance agent, policy number, and location of policy):

_____
_____
_____

☐ Other insurance policies (list type, company & agent, policy number, and location of policy):

_____
_____
_____

☐ Other: (list other documents such as stock certificates, bonds, certificates of deposit, etc., and their location):

_____
_____
_____

5. **Location of Assets.** In addition to items readily visible in my home or listed above, I have the following assets:

☐ Safe deposit box located at _____, box number _____.
Key located at: _____.

☐ Bank accounts (list name & address of bank, type of account, and account number):

_____
_____
_____
_____

☐   Other (describe the item and give its location):

_____
_____
_____

6. Other desires or information (state any desires or provide any information not given above; use additional sheets of paper if necessary):

_____
_____
_____.

Dated: _____   _____
Signature

Simple Will—Spouse and Minor Children—One Guardian

Last Will and Testament

I, _____ a resident of _____ County, _____ do hereby make, publish, and declare this to be my Last Will and Testament, hereby revoking any and all Wills and Codicils heretofore made by me.

FIRST: I direct that all my just debts and funeral expenses be paid out of my estate as soon after my death as is practicable.

SECOND: I give, devise, and bequeath the following specific gifts:

_____
_____
_____
_____
_____
_____
_____
_____
_____
_____
_____
_____
_____
_____
_____
_____

THIRD: I give, devise, and bequeath all my estate, real, personal, and mixed, of whatever kind and wherever situated, of which I may die seized or possessed, or in which I may have any interest or over which I may have any power of appointment or testamentary disposition, to my spouse, _____. If my said spouse does not survive me, I give, and bequeath the said property to my children _____ _____, plus any afterborn or adopted children in equal shares or their lineal descendants, per stirpes.

FOURTH: In the event that any beneficiary fails to survive me by thirty days, then this will shall take effect as if that person had predeceased me.

FIFTH: Should my spouse not survive me, I hereby nominate, constitute, and appoint _____ as guardian over the person and estate of any of my children who have not reached the age of majority at the time of my death. In the event that said guardian is unable or unwilling to serve, then I nominate, constitute, and appoint _____ as guardian. Said guardian shall serve without bond or surety.

Initials: _____ _____ _____ _____   Page ____ of ____
     Testator   Witness   Witness   Witness

SIXTH: I hereby nominate, constitute, and appoint _____
as Executor or Personal Representative of this, my Last Will and Testament. In the event that such named person is unable or unwilling to serve at any time or for any reason, then I nominate, constitute, and appoint _____
as Executor or Personal Representative in the place and stead of the person first named herein. It is my will and I direct that my Executor or Personal Representative shall not be required to furnish a bond for the faithful performance of his or her duties in any jurisdiction, any provision of law to the contrary notwithstanding, and I give my Executor or Personal Representative full power to administer my estate, including the power to settle claims, pay debts, and sell, lease or exchange real and personal property without court order.

IN WITNESS WHEREOF I declare this to be my Last Will and Testament and execute it willingly as my free and voluntary act for the purposes expressed herein and I am of legal age and sound mind and make this under no constraint or undue influence, this _____ day of _____, 20____ at _____
State of _____.

_____

The foregoing instrument was on said date subscribed at the end thereof by _____, the above named Testator who signed, published, and declared this instrument to be his/her Last Will and Testament in the presence of us and each of us, who thereupon at his/her request, in his/her presence, and in the presence of each other, have hereunto subscribed our names as witnesses thereto. We are of sound mind and proper age to witness a will and understand this to be his/her will, and to the best of our knowledge testator is of legal age to make a will, of sound mind, and under no constraint or undue influence.

_____ residing at _____

_____ residing at _____

_____ residing at _____

Simple Will—Spouse and Minor Children—Two Guardians

Last Will and Testament

I, _____ a resident of _____
County, _____ do hereby make, publish, and declare this to be my
Last Will and Testament, hereby revoking any and all Wills and Codicils heretofore
made by me.

FIRST: I direct that all my just debts and funeral expenses be paid out of my estate as
soon after my death as is practicable.

SECOND: I give, devise, and bequeath the following specific gifts:

_____
_____
_____
_____
_____
_____
_____
_____
_____
_____
_____
_____
_____
_____
_____

THIRD: I give, devise, and bequeath all my estate, real, personal, and mixed, of
whatever kind and wherever situated, of which I may die seized or possessed, or in
which I may have any interest or over which I may have any power of appointment or
testamentary disposition, to my spouse, _____.
If my said spouse does not survive me, I give, and bequeath the said property to my
children _____
_____, plus any
afterborn or adopted children in equal shares or their lineal descendants, per stirpes.

FOURTH: In the event that any beneficiary fails to survive me by thirty days, then this
will shall take effect as if that person had predeceased me.

FIFTH: Should my spouse not survive me, I hereby nominate, constitute, and appoint
_____, as guardian over the person of any of my
children who have not reached the age of majority at the time of my death. In the event
that said guardian is unable or unwilling to serve, then I nominate, constitute, and
appoint _____ as guardian. Said guardian shall serve
without bond or surety.

Initials: _____ _____ _____ _____   Page ____ of _____
         Testator   Witness   Witness   Witness

SIXTH: Should my spouse not survive me, I hereby nominate, constitute, and appoint _____ as guardian over the estate of any of my children who have not reached the age of majority at the time of my death. In the event that said guardian is unable or unwilling to serve, then I nominate, constitute, and appoint _____ as guardian. Said guardian shall serve without bond or surety.

SEVENTH: I hereby nominate, constitute, and appoint _____ as Executor or Personal Representative of this, my Last Will and Testament. In the event that such named person is unable or unwilling to serve at any time or for any reason, then I nominate, constitute, and appoint _____ as Executor or Personal Representative in the place and stead of the person first named herein. It is my will and I direct that my Executor or Personal Representative shall not be required to furnish a bond for the faithful performance of his or her duties in any jurisdiction, any provision of law to the contrary notwithstanding, and I give my Executor or Personal Representative full power to administer my estate, including the power to settle claims, pay debts, and sell, lease or exchange real and personal property without court order.

IN WITNESS WHEREOF I declare this to be my Last Will and Testament and execute it willingly as my free and voluntary act for the purposes expressed herein and I am of legal age and sound mind and make this under no constraint or undue influence, this _____ day of _____, 20____ at _____ State of _____.

_____

The foregoing instrument was on said date subscribed at the end thereof by _____, the above named Testator who signed, published, and declared this instrument to be his/her Last Will and Testament in the presence of us and each of us, who thereupon at his/her request, in his/her presence, and in the presence of each other, have hereunto subscribed our names as witnesses thereto. We are of sound mind and proper age to witness a will and understand this to be his/her will, and to the best of our knowledge testator is of legal age to make a will, of sound mind, and under no constraint or undue influence.

_____ residing at _____

_____ residing at _____

_____ residing at _____

Simple Will—Spouse and Minor Children—Guardian and Trust

Last Will and Testament

I, _____ a resident of _____ County, _____ do hereby make, publish, and declare this to be my Last Will and Testament, hereby revoking any and all Wills and Codicils heretofore made by me.

FIRST: I direct that all my just debts and funeral expenses be paid out of my estate as soon after my death as is practicable.

SECOND: I give, devise, and bequeath the following specific gifts:

_____
_____
_____
_____
_____
_____
_____
_____
_____

THIRD: I give, devise, and bequeath all my estate, real, personal, and mixed, of whatever kind and wherever situated, of which I may die seized or possessed, or in which I may have any interest or over which I may have any power of appointment or testamentary disposition, to my spouse, _____. If my said spouse does not survive me, I give, and bequeath the said property to my children _____ _____, plus any afterborn or adopted children in equal shares or their lineal descendants, per stirpes.

FOURTH: In the event that any beneficiary fails to survive me by thirty days, then this will shall take effect as if that person had predeceased me.

FIFTH: In the event that any of my children have not reached the age of _____ years at the time of my death, then the share of any such child shall be held in a separate trust by _____ for such child.

The trustee shall use the income and that part of the principal of the trust as is, in the trustee's sole discretion, necessary or desirable to provide proper housing, medical care, food, clothing, entertainment and education for the trust beneficiary, considering the beneficiary's other resources. Any income that is not distributed shall be added to the principal. Additionally, the trustee shall have all powers conferred by the law of the state having jurisdiction over this trust, as well as the power to pay from the assets of the trust reasonable fees necessary to administer the trust.

The trust shall terminate when the child reaches the age specified above and the remaining assets distributed to the child, unless they have been exhausted sooner. In the event the child dies prior to the termination of the trust, then the assets shall pass to the estate of the child. The interests of the beneficiary under this trust shall not be assignable and shall be free from the claims of creditors to the full extent allowed by law.

In the event the said trustee is unable or unwilling to serve for any reason, then I nominate, constitute, and appoint _____ as alternate trustee. No bond shall be required of either trustee in any jurisdiction and this trust shall be administered without court supervision as allowed by law.

SIXTH: Should my spouse not survive me, I hereby nominate, constitute, and appoint _____ as guardian over the person and estate of any of my children who have not reached the age of majority at the time of my death. In the event that said guardian is unable or unwilling to serve, then I nominate, constitute, and appoint _____ as guardian.

SEVENTH: I hereby nominate, constitute, and appoint _____ as Executor or Personal Representative of this, my Last Will and Testament. In the event that such named person is unable or unwilling to serve at any time or for any reason, then I nominate, constitute, and appoint _____ as Executor or Personal Representative in the place and stead of the person first named herein. It is my will and I direct that my Executor or Personal Representative shall not be required to furnish a bond for the faithful performance of his or her duties in any jurisdiction, any provision of law to the contrary notwithstanding, and I give my Executor or Personal Representative full power to administer my estate, including the power to settle claims, pay debts, and sell, lease or exchange real and personal property without court order.

IN WITNESS WHEREOF I declare this to be my Last Will and Testament and execute it willingly as my free and voluntary act for the purposes expressed herein and I am of legal age and sound mind and make this under no constraint or undue influence, this _____ day of _____, 20____ at _____ State of _____.

_____

The foregoing instrument was on said date subscribed at the end thereof by _____, the above named Testator who signed, published, and declared this instrument to be his/her Last Will and Testament in the presence of us and each of us, who thereupon at his/her request, in his/her presence, and in the presence of each other, have hereunto subscribed our names as witnesses thereto. We are of sound mind and proper age to witness a will and understand this to be his/her will, and to the best of our knowledge testator is of legal age to make a will, of sound mind, and under no constraint or undue influence.

_____ residing at _____

_____ residing at _____

_____ residing at _____

Simple Will—Spouse and No Children (Survivor)

Last Will and Testament

I, _____ a resident of _____
County, _____ do hereby make, publish, and declare this to be my
Last Will and Testament, hereby revoking any and all Wills and Codicils heretofore
made by me.

FIRST: I direct that all my just debts and funeral expenses be paid out of my estate as
soon after my death as is practicable.

SECOND: I give, devise, and bequeath the following specific gifts:

_____
_____
_____
_____
_____
_____
_____
_____
_____
_____
_____
_____
_____
_____
_____

THIRD: I give, devise, and bequeath all my estate, real, personal, and mixed, of
whatever kind and wherever situated, of which I may die seized or possessed, or in
which I may have any interest or over which I may have any power of appointment or
testamentary disposition, to my spouse, _____.
If my said spouse does not survive me, I give, and bequeath the said property to

_____
_____
_____
_____, or the survivor of them.

FOURTH: In the event that any beneficiary fails to survive me by thirty days, then this
will shall take effect as if that person had predeceased me.

FIFTH: I hereby nominate, constitute, and appoint _____
as Executor or Personal Representative of this, my Last Will and Testament. In the
event that such named person is unable or unwilling to serve at any time or for any
reason, then I nominate, constitute, and appoint _____
as Executor or Personal Representative in the place and stead of the person first
named herein. It is my will and I direct that my Executor or Personal Representative

Initials: _____ _____ _____ _____   Page ____ of _____
     Testator   Witness   Witness   Witness

shall not be required to furnish a bond for the faithful performance of his or her duties in any jurisdiction, any provision of law to the contrary notwithstanding, and I give my Executor or Personal Representative full power to administer my estate, including the power to settle claims, pay debts, and sell, lease or exchange real and personal property without court order.

IN WITNESS WHEREOF I declare this to be my Last Will and Testament and execute it willingly as my free and voluntary act for the purposes expressed herein and I am of legal age and sound mind and make this under no constraint or undue influence, this _____ day of _____, 20_____ at _____ State of _____.

_____

The foregoing instrument was on said date subscribed at the end thereof by _____, the above named Testator who signed, published, and declared this instrument to be his/her Last Will and Testament in the presence of us and each of us, who thereupon at his/her request, in his/her presence, and in the presence of each other, have hereunto subscribed our names as witnesses thereto. We are of sound mind and proper age to witness a will and understand this to be his/her will, and to the best of our knowledge testator is of legal age to make a will, of sound mind, and under no constraint or undue influence.

_____ residing at _____

_____ residing at _____

_____ residing at _____

Simple Will—Spouse and No Children (Others or Their Descendants)

Last Will and Testament

I, _____ a resident of _____ County, _____ do hereby make, publish, and declare this to be my Last Will and Testament, hereby revoking any and all Wills and Codicils heretofore made by me.

FIRST: I direct that all my just debts and funeral expenses be paid out of my estate as soon after my death as is practicable.

SECOND: I give, devise, and bequeath the following specific gifts:

_____
_____
_____
_____
_____
_____
_____
_____
_____
_____
_____
_____
_____
_____
_____

THIRD: I give, devise, and bequeath all my estate, real, personal, and mixed, of whatever kind and wherever situated, of which I may die seized or possessed, or in which I may have any interest or over which I may have any power of appointment or testamentary disposition, to my spouse, _____. If my said spouse does not survive me, I give, and bequeath the said property to

_____
_____
_____
_____, or to their lineal descendants, per stirpes.

FOURTH: In the event that any beneficiary fails to survive me by thirty days, then this will shall take effect as if that person had predeceased me.

FIFTH: I hereby nominate, constitute, and appoint _____ as Executor or Personal Representative of this, my Last Will and Testament. In the event that such named person is unable or unwilling to serve at any time or for any reason, then I nominate, constitute, and appoint _____ as Executor or Personal Representative in the place and stead of the person first named herein. It is my will and I direct that my Executor or Personal Representative

Initials: _____ _____ _____ _____   Page ____ of ____
         Testator   Witness   Witness   Witness

shall not be required to furnish a bond for the faithful performance of his or her duties in any jurisdiction, any provision of law to the contrary notwithstanding, and I give my Executor or Personal Representative full power to administer my estate, including the power to settle claims, pay debts, and sell, lease or exchange real and personal property without court order.

IN WITNESS WHEREOF I declare this to be my Last Will and Testament and execute it willingly as my free and voluntary act for the purposes expressed herein and I am of legal age and sound mind and make this under no constraint or undue influence, this _____ day of _____, 20_____ at _____ State of _____.

_____

The foregoing instrument was on said date subscribed at the end thereof by _____, the above named Testator who signed, published, and declared this instrument to be his/her Last Will and Testament in the presence of us and each of us, who thereupon at his/her request, in his/her presence, and in the presence of each other, have hereunto subscribed our names as witnesses thereto. We are of sound mind and proper age to witness a will and understand this to be his/her will, and to the best of our knowledge testator is of legal age to make a will, of sound mind, and under no constraint or undue influence.

_____ residing at _____

_____ residing at _____

_____ residing at _____

Simple Will—Spouse and Adult Children (All to Spouse)

Last Will and Testament

I, _____ a resident of _____ County, _____ do hereby make, publish, and declare this to be my Last Will and Testament, hereby revoking any and all Wills and Codicils heretofore made by me.

FIRST: I direct that all my just debts and funeral expenses be paid out of my estate as soon after my death as is practicable.

SECOND: I give, devise, and bequeath the following specific gifts:

_____

_____

_____

_____

_____

_____

_____

_____

_____

_____

_____

_____

_____

_____

_____

THIRD: I give, devise, and bequeath all my estate, real, personal, and mixed, of whatever kind and wherever situated, of which I may die seized or possessed, or in which I may have any interest or over which I may have any power of appointment or testamentary disposition, to my spouse, _____. If my said spouse does not survive me, I give, and bequeath the said property to my children _____

_____

_____, in equal shares or to their lineal descendants, per stirpes.

FOURTH: In the event that any beneficiary fails to survive me by thirty days, then this will shall take effect as if that person had predeceased me.

FIFTH: I hereby nominate, constitute, and appoint _____ as Executor or Personal Representative of this, my Last Will and Testament. In the event that such named person is unable or unwilling to serve at any time or for any reason, then I nominate, constitute, and appoint _____ as Executor or Personal Representative in the place and stead of the person first named herein. It is my will and I direct that my Executor or Personal Representative

shall not be required to furnish a bond for the faithful performance of his or her duties in any jurisdiction, any provision of law to the contrary notwithstanding, and I give my Executor or Personal Representative full power to administer my estate, including the power to settle claims, pay debts, and sell, lease or exchange real and personal property without court order.

IN WITNESS WHEREOF I declare this to be my Last Will and Testament and execute it willingly as my free and voluntary act for the purposes expressed herein and I am of legal age and sound mind and make this under no constraint or undue influence, this _____ day of _____, 20____ at _____ State of _____.

_____

The foregoing instrument was on said date subscribed at the end thereof by _____, the above named Testator who signed, published, and declared this instrument to be his/her Last Will and Testament in the presence of us and each of us, who thereupon at his/her request, in his/her presence, and in the presence of each other, have hereunto subscribed our names as witnesses thereto. We are of sound mind and proper age to witness a will and understand this to be his/her will, and to the best of our knowledge testator is of legal age to make a will, of sound mind, and under no constraint or undue influence.

_____ residing at _____

_____ residing at _____

_____ residing at _____

form 9   163

Simple Will—Spouse and Adult Children (To Spouse and Children)

Last Will and Testament

I, _____ a resident of _____
County, _____ do hereby make, publish, and declare this to be my
Last Will and Testament, hereby revoking any and all Wills and Codicils heretofore
made by me.

FIRST: I direct that all my just debts and funeral expenses be paid out of my estate as
soon after my death as is practicable.

SECOND: I give, devise, and bequeath the following specific gifts:

_____
_____
_____
_____
_____
_____
_____
_____
_____
_____
_____
_____
_____
_____
_____
_____

THIRD: I give, devise, and bequeath all my estate, real, personal, and mixed, of
whatever kind and wherever situated, of which I may die seized or possessed, or in
which I may have any interest or over which I may have any power of appointment or
testamentary disposition, as follows:
_____% to my spouse, _____ and
_____% to my children, _____
_____
_____
_____, in equal shares or to their lineal descendants per stirpes.

FOURTH: In the event that any beneficiary fails to survive me by thirty days, then this
will shall take effect as if that person had predeceased me.

FIFTH: I hereby nominate, constitute, and appoint _____
as Executor or Personal Representative of this, my Last Will and Testament. In the
event that such named person is unable or unwilling to serve at any time or for any
reason, then I nominate, constitute, and appoint _____
as Executor or Personal Representative in the place and stead of the person first
named herein. It is my will and I direct that my Executor or Personal Representative

Initials: _____ _____ _____ _____   Page ____ of ____
         Testator   Witness   Witness   Witness

shall not be required to furnish a bond for the faithful performance of his or her duties in any jurisdiction, any provision of law to the contrary notwithstanding, and I give my Executor or Personal Representative full power to administer my estate, including the power to settle claims, pay debts, and sell, lease or exchange real and personal property without court order.

IN WITNESS WHEREOF I declare this to be my Last Will and Testament and execute it willingly as my free and voluntary act for the purposes expressed herein and I am of legal age and sound mind and make this under no constraint or undue influence, this _____ day of _____, 20____ at _____ State of _____.

_____

The foregoing instrument was on said date subscribed at the end thereof by _____, the above named Testator who signed, published, and declared this instrument to be his/her Last Will and Testament in the presence of us and each of us, who thereupon at his/her request, in his/her presence, and in the presence of each other, have hereunto subscribed our names as witnesses thereto. We are of sound mind and proper age to witness a will and understand this to be his/her will, and to the best of our knowledge testator is of legal age to make a will, of sound mind, and under no constraint or undue influence.

_____ residing at _____

_____ residing at _____

_____ residing at _____

Simple Will—No Spouse—Minor Children—One Guardian

Last Will and Testament

I, _____ a resident of _____ County, _____ do hereby make, publish, and declare this to be my Last Will and Testament, hereby revoking any and all Wills and Codicils heretofore made by me.

FIRST: I direct that all my just debts and funeral expenses be paid out of my estate as soon after my death as is practicable.

SECOND: I give, devise, and bequeath the following specific gifts:

_____
_____
_____
_____
_____
_____
_____
_____
_____
_____
_____
_____
_____
_____
_____
_____

THIRD: I give, devise, and bequeath all my estate, real, personal, and mixed, of whatever kind and wherever situated, of which I may die seized or possessed, or in which I may have any interest or over which I may have any power of appointment or testamentary disposition, to my children _____

_____

_____, plus any afterborn or adopted children in equal shares or to their lineal descendants per stirpes.

FOURTH: In the event that any beneficiary fails to survive me by thirty days, then this will shall take effect as if that person had predeceased me.

FIFTH: In the event any of my children have not attained the age of 18 years at the time of my death, I hereby nominate, constitute, and appoint _____ as guardian over the person and estate of any of my children who have not reached the age of majority at the time of my death. In the event that said guardian is unable or unwilling to serve, then I nominate, constitute, and appoint _____ as guardian. Said guardian shall serve without bond or surety.

Initials: _____ _____ _____ _____   Page ____ of ____
       Testator   Witness   Witness   Witness

SIXTH: I hereby nominate, constitute, and appoint _____
as Executor or Personal Representative of this, my Last Will and Testament. In the event that such named person is unable or unwilling to serve at any time or for any reason, then I nominate, constitute, and appoint _____
as Executor or Personal Representative in the place and stead of the person first named herein. It is my will and I direct that my Executor or Personal Representative shall not be required to furnish a bond for the faithful performance of his or her duties in any jurisdiction, any provision of law to the contrary notwithstanding, and I give my Executor or Personal Representative full power to administer my estate, including the power to settle claims, pay debts, and sell, lease or exchange real and personal property without court order.

IN WITNESS WHEREOF I declare this to be my Last Will and Testament and execute it willingly as my free and voluntary act for the purposes expressed herein and I am of legal age and sound mind and make this under no constraint or undue influence, this _____ day of _____, 20____ at _____ State of _____.

_____

The foregoing instrument was on said date subscribed at the end thereof by _____, the above named Testator who signed, published, and declared this instrument to be his/her Last Will and Testament in the presence of us and each of us, who thereupon at his/her request, in his/her presence, and in the presence of each other, have hereunto subscribed our names as witnesses thereto. We are of sound mind and proper age to witness a will and understand this to be his/her will, and to the best of our knowledge testator is of legal age to make a will, of sound mind, and under no constraint or undue influence.

_____ residing at _____

_____ residing at _____

_____ residing at _____

Simple Will—No Spouse—Minor Children—Guardian Over Persons, Guardian Over Property

Last Will and Testament

I, _____ a resident of _____
County, _____ do hereby make, publish, and declare this to be my Last Will and Testament, hereby revoking any and all Wills and Codicils heretofore made by me.

FIRST: I direct that all my just debts and funeral expenses be paid out of my estate as soon after my death as is practicable.

SECOND: I give, devise, and bequeath the following specific gifts:
_____
_____
_____
_____
_____
_____
_____
_____
_____
_____
_____
_____
_____
_____
_____
_____
_____
_____

THIRD: I give, devise, and bequeath all my estate, real, personal, and mixed, of whatever kind and wherever situated, of which I may die seized or possessed, or in which I may have any interest or over which I may have any power of appointment or testamentary disposition, to my children _____
_____
_____
_____, plus any afterborn or adopted children in equal shares or to their lineal descendants per stirpes.

FOURTH: In the event that any beneficiary fails to survive me by thirty days, then this will shall take effect as if that person had predeceased me.

FIFTH: In the event any of my children have not attained the age of 18 years at the time of my death, I hereby nominate, constitute, and appoint _____
as guardian over the person of any of my children who have not reached the age of majority at the time of my death. In the event that said guardian is unable or unwilling to serve, then I nominate, constitute, and appoint _____
as guardian. Said guardian shall serve without bond or surety.

Initials: _____   _____   _____   _____   Page ____ of _____
    Testator   Witness   Witness   Witness

SIXTH: In the event any of my children have not attained the age of 18 years at the time of my death, I hereby nominate, constitute, and appoint _____ as guardian over the estate of any of my children who have not reached the age of majority at the time of my death. In the event that said guardian is unable or unwilling to serve, then I nominate, constitute, and appoint _____ as guardian. Said guardian shall serve without bond or surety.

SEVENTH: I hereby nominate, constitute, and appoint _____ as Executor or Personal Representative of this, my Last Will and Testament. In the event that such named person is unable or unwilling to serve at any time or for any reason, then I nominate, constitute, and appoint _____ as Executor or Personal Representative in the place and stead of the person first named herein. It is my will and I direct that my Executor or Personal Representative shall not be required to furnish a bond for the faithful performance of his or her duties in any jurisdiction, any provision of law to the contrary notwithstanding, and I give my Executor or Personal Representative full power to administer my estate, including the power to settle claims, pay debts, and sell, lease or exchange real and personal property without court order.

IN WITNESS WHEREOF I declare this to be my Last Will and Testament and execute it willingly as my free and voluntary act for the purposes expressed herein and I am of legal age and sound mind and make this under no constraint or undue influence, this _____ day of _____, 20____ at _____ State of _____.

_____

The foregoing instrument was on said date subscribed at the end thereof by _____, the above named Testator who signed, published, and declared this instrument to be his/her Last Will and Testament in the presence of us and each of us, who thereupon at his/her request, in his/her presence, and in the presence of each other, have hereunto subscribed our names as witnesses thereto. We are of sound mind and proper age to witness a will and understand this to be his/her will, and to the best of our knowledge testator is of legal age to make a will, of sound mind, and under no constraint or undue influence.

_____ residing at _____

_____ residing at _____

_____ residing at _____

Simple Will—No Spouse—Minor Children—Guardian and Trust

Last Will and Testament

I, _____ a resident of _____ County, _____ do hereby make, publish, and declare this to be my Last Will and Testament, hereby revoking any and all Wills and Codicils heretofore made by me.

FIRST: I direct that all my just debts and funeral expenses be paid out of my estate as soon after my death as is practicable.

SECOND: I give, devise, and bequeath the following specific gifts:

_____

_____

_____

_____

_____

_____

_____

_____

THIRD: I give, devise, and bequeath all my estate, real, personal, and mixed, of whatever kind and wherever situated, of which I may die seized or possessed, or in which I may have any interest or over which I may have any power of appointment or testamentary disposition, to my children _____

_____, plus any afterborn or adopted children in equal shares or to their lineal descendants per stirpes.

FOURTH: In the event that any beneficiary fails to survive me by thirty days, then this will shall take effect as if that person had predeceased me.

FIFTH: In the event that any of my children have not reached the age of _____ years at the time of my death, then the share of any such child shall be held in a separate trust by _____ for such child.

The trustee shall use the income and that part of the principal of the trust as is, in the trustee's sole discretion, necessary or desirable to provide proper housing, medical care, food, clothing, entertainment and education for the trust beneficiary, considering the beneficiary's other resources. Any income that is not distributed shall be added to the principal. Additionally, the trustee shall have all powers conferred by the law of the state having jurisdiction over this trust, as well as the power to pay from the assets of the trust reasonable fees necessary to administer the trust.

The trust shall terminate when the child reaches the age specified above and the remaining assets distributed to the child, unless they have been exhausted sooner. In the event the child dies prior to the termination of the trust, then the assets shall pass to the estate of the child. The interests of the beneficiary under this trust shall not be assignable and shall be free from the claims of creditors to the full extent allowed by law.

In the event the said trustee is unable or unwilling to serve for any reason, then I nominate, constitute, and appoint _____as alternate trustee. No bond shall be required of either trustee in any jurisdiction and this trust shall be administered without court supervision as allowed by law.

SIXTH: In the event any of my children have not attained the age of 18 years at the time of my death, I hereby nominate, constitute, and appoint _____ as guardian over the person and estate of any of my children who have not reached the age of majority at the time of my death. In the event that said guardian is unable or unwilling to serve, then I nominate, constitute, and appoint _____ as guardian. Said guardian shall serve without bond or surety.

SEVENTH: I hereby nominate, constitute, and appoint _____ as Executor or Personal Representative of this, my Last Will and Testament. In the event that such named person is unable or unwilling to serve at any time or for any reason, then I nominate, constitute, and appoint _____ as Executor or Personal Representative in the place and stead of the person first named herein. It is my will and I direct that my Executor or Personal Representative shall not be required to furnish a bond for the faithful performance of his or her duties in any jurisdiction, any provision of law to the contrary notwithstanding, and I give my Executor or Personal Representative full power to administer my estate, including the power to settle claims, pay debts, and sell, lease or exchange real and personal property without court order.

IN WITNESS WHEREOF I declare this to be my Last Will and Testament and execute it willingly as my free and voluntary act for the purposes expressed herein and I am of legal age and sound mind and make this under no constraint or undue influence, this _____ day of _____, 20____ at _____ State of _____.

_____

The foregoing instrument was on said date subscribed at the end thereof by _____, the above named Testator who signed, published, and declared this instrument to be his/her Last Will and Testament in the presence of us and each of us, who thereupon at his/her request, in his/her presence, and in the presence of each other, have hereunto subscribed our names as witnesses thereto. We are of sound mind and proper age to witness a will and understand this to be his/her will, and to the best of our knowledge testator is of legal age to make a will, of sound mind, and under no constraint or undue influence.

_____ residing at _____

_____ residing at _____

_____ residing at _____

Simple Will—No Spouse—Adult Children (Equal by Family)

Last Will and Testament

I, _____ a resident of _____
County, _____ do hereby make, publish, and declare this to be my
Last Will and Testament, hereby revoking any and all Wills and Codicils heretofore
made by me.

FIRST: I direct that all my just debts and funeral expenses be paid out of my estate as
soon after my death as is practicable.

SECOND: I give, devise, and bequeath the following specific gifts:

_____
_____
_____
_____
_____
_____
_____
_____
_____
_____
_____

THIRD: I give, devise, and bequeath all my estate, real, personal, and mixed, of
whatever kind and wherever situated, of which I may die seized or possessed, or in
which I may have any interest or over which I may have any power of appointment or
testamentary disposition, to my children _____
_____
_____, in equal shares, or their lineal descendants per stirpes.

FOURTH: In the event that any beneficiary fails to survive me by thirty days, then this
will shall take effect as if that person had predeceased me.

FIFTH: I hereby nominate, constitute, and appoint _____
as Executor or Personal Representative of this, my Last Will and Testament. In the
event that such named person is unable or unwilling to serve at any time or for any
reason, then I nominate, constitute, and appoint _____
as Executor or Personal Representative in the place and stead of the person first
named herein. It is my will and I direct that my Executor or Personal Representative
shall not be required to furnish a bond for the faithful performance of his or her duties in
any jurisdiction, any provision of law to the contrary notwithstanding, and I give my
Executor or Personal Representative full power to administer my estate, including the
power to settle claims, pay debts, and sell, lease or exchange real and personal
property without court order.

Initials: _____ _____ _____ _____   Page _____ of _____
　　　　　 Testator　　 Witness　　　Witness　　　Witness

IN WITNESS WHEREOF I declare this to be my Last Will and Testament and execute it willingly as my free and voluntary act for the purposes expressed herein and I am of legal age and sound mind and make this under no constraint or undue influence, this _____ day of _____, 20_____ at _____
State of _____.

_____

The foregoing instrument was on said date subscribed at the end thereof by _____, the above named Testator who signed, published, and declared this instrument to be his/her Last Will and Testament in the presence of us and each of us, who thereupon at his/her request, in his/her presence, and in the presence of each other, have hereunto subscribed our names as witnesses thereto. We are of sound mind and proper age to witness a will and understand this to be his/her will, and to the best of our knowledge testator is of legal age to make a will, of sound mind, and under no constraint or undue influence.

_____ residing at _____

_____ residing at _____

_____ residing at _____

Simple Will—No Spouse—Adult Children (Equal by Person)

Last Will and Testament

I, _____ a resident of _____ County, _____ do hereby make, publish, and declare this to be my Last Will and Testament, hereby revoking any and all Wills and Codicils heretofore made by me.

FIRST: I direct that all my just debts and funeral expenses be paid out of my estate as soon after my death as is practicable.

SECOND: I give, devise, and bequeath the following specific gifts:

_____

_____

_____

_____

_____

_____

_____

_____

_____

_____

_____

THIRD: I give, devise, and bequeath all my estate, real, personal, and mixed, of whatever kind and wherever situated, of which I may die seized or possessed, or in which I may have any interest or over which I may have any power of appointment or testamentary disposition, to my children _____

_____

_____

_____, in equal shares, or their lineal descendants per capita.

FOURTH: In the event that any beneficiary fails to survive me by thirty days, then this will shall take effect as if that person had predeceased me.

FIFTH: I hereby nominate, constitute, and appoint _____ as Executor or Personal Representative of this, my Last Will and Testament. In the event that such named person is unable or unwilling to serve at any time or for any reason, then I nominate, constitute, and appoint _____ as Executor or Personal Representative in the place and stead of the person first named herein. It is my will and I direct that my Executor or Personal Representative shall not be required to furnish a bond for the faithful performance of his or her duties in any jurisdiction, any provision of law to the contrary notwithstanding, and I give my Executor or Personal Representative full power to administer my estate, including the power to settle claims, pay debts, and sell, lease or exchange real and personal property without court order.

Initials: _____	_____	_____	_____	Page ____ of _____
Testator	Witness	Witness	Witness	

IN WITNESS WHEREOF I declare this to be my Last Will and Testament and execute it willingly as my free and voluntary act for the purposes expressed herein and I am of legal age and sound mind and make this under no constraint or undue influence, this _____ day of _____, 20_____ at _____ State of _____.

_____

The foregoing instrument was on said date subscribed at the end thereof by _____, the above named Testator who signed, published, and declared this instrument to be his/her Last Will and Testament in the presence of us and each of us, who thereupon at his/her request, in his/her presence, and in the presence of each other, have hereunto subscribed our names as witnesses thereto. We are of sound mind and proper age to witness a will and understand this to be his/her will, and to the best of our knowledge testator is of legal age to make a will, of sound mind, and under no constraint or undue influence.

_____ residing at _____

_____ residing at _____

_____ residing at _____

Simple Will—No Spouse and No Children (To Survivor)

Last Will and Testament

I, _____ a resident of _____ County, _____ do hereby make, publish, and declare this to be my Last Will and Testament, hereby revoking any and all Wills and Codicils heretofore made by me.

FIRST: I direct that all my just debts and funeral expenses be paid out of my estate as soon after my death as is practicable.

SECOND: I give, devise, and bequeath the following specific gifts:

_____

_____

_____

_____

_____

_____

_____

_____

_____

THIRD: I give, devise, and bequeath all my estate, real, personal, and mixed, of whatever kind and wherever situated, of which I may die seized or possessed, or in which I may have any interest or over which I may have any power of appointment or testamentary disposition, to the following: _____

_____

_____, in equal share, or to the survivor of them.

FOURTH: In the event that any beneficiary fails to survive me by thirty days, then this will shall take effect as if that person had predeceased me.

FIFTH: I hereby nominate, constitute, and appoint _____ as Executor or Personal Representative of this, my Last Will and Testament. In the event that such named person is unable or unwilling to serve at any time or for any reason, then I nominate, constitute, and appoint _____ as Executor or Personal Representative in the place and stead of the person first named herein. It is my will and I direct that my Executor or Personal Representative shall not be required to furnish a bond for the faithful performance of his or her duties in any jurisdiction, any provision of law to the contrary notwithstanding, and I give my Executor or Personal Representative full power to administer my estate, including the power to settle claims, pay debts, and sell, lease or exchange real and personal property without court order.

Initials: _____ _____ _____ _____   Page ____ of ____
      Testator   Witness   Witness   Witness

IN WITNESS WHEREOF I declare this to be my Last Will and Testament and execute it willingly as my free and voluntary act for the purposes expressed herein and I am of legal age and sound mind and make this under no constraint or undue influence, this _____ day of _____, 20____ at _____
State of _____.

_____

The foregoing instrument was on said date subscribed at the end thereof by _____, the above named Testator who signed, published, and declared this instrument to be his/her Last Will and Testament in the presence of us and each of us, who thereupon at his/her request, in his/her presence, and in the presence of each other, have hereunto subscribed our names as witnesses thereto. We are of sound mind and proper age to witness a will and understand this to be his/her will, and to the best of our knowledge testator is of legal age to make a will, of sound mind, and under no constraint or undue influence.

_____ residing at _____

_____ residing at _____

_____ residing at _____

Simple Will—No Spouse and No Children (To Descendants)

Last Will and Testament

I, _____ a resident of _____ County, _____ do hereby make, publish, and declare this to be my Last Will and Testament, hereby revoking any and all Wills and Codicils heretofore made by me.

FIRST: I direct that all my just debts and funeral expenses be paid out of my estate as soon after my death as is practicable.

SECOND: I give, devise, and bequeath the following specific gifts:

_____

_____

_____

_____

_____

_____

_____

_____

_____

_____

THIRD: I give, devise, and bequeath all my estate, real, personal, and mixed, of whatever kind and wherever situated, of which I may die seized or possessed, or in which I may have any interest or over which I may have any power of appointment or testamentary disposition, to the following: _____

_____

_____, in equal shares, or their lineal descendants per stirpes.

FOURTH: In the event that any beneficiary fails to survive me by thirty days, then this will shall take effect as if that person had predeceased me.

FIFTH: I hereby nominate, constitute, and appoint _____ as Executor or Personal Representative of this, my Last Will and Testament. In the event that such named person is unable or unwilling to serve at any time or for any reason, then I nominate, constitute, and appoint _____ as Executor or Personal Representative in the place and stead of the person first named herein. It is my will and I direct that my Executor or Personal Representative shall not be required to furnish a bond for the faithful performance of his or her duties in any jurisdiction, any provision of law to the contrary notwithstanding, and I give my Executor or Personal Representative full power to administer my estate, including the power to settle claims, pay debts, and sell, lease or exchange real and personal property without court order.

Initials: _____ _____ _____ _____   Page ____ of _____
         Testator   Witness   Witness   Witness

IN WITNESS WHEREOF I declare this to be my Last Will and Testament and execute it willingly as my free and voluntary act for the purposes expressed herein and I am of legal age and sound mind and make this under no constraint or undue influence, this _____ day of _____, 20____ at _____ State of _____.

_____

The foregoing instrument was on said date subscribed at the end thereof by _____, the above named Testator who signed, published, and declared this instrument to be his/her Last Will and Testament in the presence of us and each of us, who thereupon at his/her request, in his/her presence, and in the presence of each other, have hereunto subscribed our names as witnesses thereto. We are of sound mind and proper age to witness a will and understand this to be his/her will, and to the best of our knowledge testator is of legal age to make a will, of sound mind, and under no constraint or undue influence.

_____ residing at _____

_____ residing at _____

_____ residing at _____

Self-Proved Will Affidavit
(attach to Will)

STATE OF _____

COUNTY OF _____

We, _____, and _____, and _____, the testator and the witnesses, whose names are signed to the attached or foregoing instrument in those capacities, personally appearing before the undersigned authority and being first duly sworn, declare to the undersigned authority under penalty of perjury that: 1) the testator declared, signed, and executed the instrument as his or her last will; 2) he or she signed it willingly, or directed another to sign for him or her; 3) he or she executed it as his or her free and voluntary act for the purposes therein expressed; and 4) each of the witnesses, at the request of the testator, in his or her hearing and presence and in the presence of each other, signed the will as witnesses, and that to the best of his or her knowledge the testator was at that time of full legal age, of sound mind, and under no constraint or undue influence.

_____ (Testator)

_____ (Witness)

_____ (Witness)

Subscribed, sworn, and acknowledged before me _____, a notary public, and by _____, the testator, and by _____ and _____, witnesses, this _____ day of _____, 20____.

_____
Notary public

This page intentionally blank.

Self-Proved Will Affidavit
(attach to Will)

STATE OF _____

COUNTY OF _____

I, the undersigned, an officer authorized to administer oaths, certify that
_____,
the testator and _____, and
_____, the witnesses, whose names
are signed to the attached or foregoing instrument and whose signatures appear below,
having appeared before me and having been first been duly sworn, each then declared
to me that: 1) the attached or foregoing instrument is the last will of the testator; 2) the
testator willingly and voluntarily declared, signed, and executed the will in the presence
of the witnesses; 3) the witnesses signed the will upon the request of the testator, in the
presence and hearing of the testator and in the presence of each other; 4) to the best
knowledge of each witness, the testator was, at the time of signing, of the age of
majority (or otherwise legally competent to make a will), of sound mind and memory,
and under no constraint or undue influence; and 5) each witness was and is competent
and of proper age to witness a will.

_____ (Testator)

_____ (Witness)

_____ (Witness)

Subscribed and sworn to before me by _____, the testator,
who is personally known to me or who has produced _____
as identification, and by _____, a witness,
who is personally known to me or who has produced _____
as identification, and by _____, a witness, who
is personally known to me or who has produced _____
as identification, this _____ day of_____, 20____.

_____
Notary or other officer

This page intentionally blank.

Notarial Will Page—Louisiana
(attach to Will)

STATE OF LOUISIANA

PARISH OF _____

The testator has signed this will at the end and on each other separate page, and has declared or signified in our presence that it is his or her last will and testament, and in the presence of the testator and each other we have hereunto subscribed our names this _____ day of _____, _____.

_____ (Testator)

_____ (Witness)

_____ (Witness)

On this _____ day of _____, _____ before me personally appeared _____, the testator, and _____, and _____, the witnesses, to me known to be the persons described in and who executed the foregoing instrument, and acknowledged that they executed it as their free act and deed.

Signed: _____
                              Notary

Note: In Louisiana a will must be signed on all pages by the testator. On page 1 replace "County" with "Parish."

This page intentionally blank.

Self-Proved Will Page—New Hampshire
(attach to Will)

The foregoing instrument was acknowledged before me this _____
by _____ the testator; _____
and _____, the witnesses, who under oath swear as
follows:

1. The testator signed the instrument as his will or expressly directed another to sign for him.

2. This was the testator's free and voluntary act for the purposes expressed in the will.

3. Each witness signed at the request of the testator, in his presence, and in the presence of the other witness.

4. To the best of my knowledge, at the time of the signing the testator was at least 18 years of age, or if under 18 years was a married person, and was of sane mind and under no constraint or undue influence.

_____
Signature

_____
Official Capacity

This page intentionally blank.

Self-Proved Will Affidavit—Texas
(attach to Will)

STATE OF TEXAS

COUNTY OF _____

Before me, the undersigned authority, on this day personally appeared _____
_____, _____, and
_____, known to me to be the testator and the
witnesses, respectively, whose names are subscribed to the annexed or foregoing
instrument in their respective capacities, and, all of said persons being by me duly
sworn, the said _____ testator, declared to me and to the
said witnesses in my presence that said instrument is his or her last will and testament,
and that he or she had willingly made and executed it as his or her free act and deed,
and the said witnesses, each on his or her oath stated to me in the presence and
hearing of the said testator, that the said testator had declared to them that said
instrument is his or her last will and testament, and that he or she executed same as
such and wanted each of them to sign it as a witness; and upon their oaths each
witness stated further that they did sign the same as witnesses in the presence of the
said testator and at his or her request; that he or she was at the time eighteen years of
age or over (or being under such age, was or had been lawfully married, or was then a
member of the armed forces of the United States or an auxiliary thereof or of the
Maritime Service) and was of sound mind; and that each of said witnesses was then at
least fourteen years of age.

_____ (Testator)

_____ (Witness)

_____ (Witness)

Subscribed and sworn to before me by _____, the testator,
and by _____, and _____,
the witnesses, this _____ day of _____, 20____.

Signed: _____

_____
Official Capacity of Officer

This page intentionally blank.

First Codicil to the Will of

_____

I, _____, a resident of _____
County, _____ declare this to be the first codicil to my Last Will and
Testament dated _____, _____.

FIRST: I hereby revoke the clause of my Will which reads as follows: _____
_____
_____
_____
_____.

SECOND: I hereby add the following clause to my Will: _____
_____
_____
_____
_____.

THIRD: In all other respects I hereby confirm and republish my Last Will and Testament
dated _____, _____.

IN WITNESS WHEREOF, I have signed, published, and declared the foregoing
instrument as and for a codicil to my Last Will and Testament, this _____ day of
_____, 20_____.

_____

The foregoing instrument was on the _____ day of _____, _____,
signed at the end thereof, and at the same time published and declared by
_____, as and for a codicil to his/her Last Will and
Testament, dated _____, 20_____, in the presence of each of us,
who, this attestation clause having been read to us, did at the request of the said
testator/testatrix, in his/her presence and in the presence of each other signed our
names as witnesses thereto.

_____ residing at _____

_____ residing at _____

_____ residing at _____

This page intentionally blank.

Self-Proved Codicil Affidavit
(attach to Codicil)

STATE OF _____

COUNTY OF _____

We, _____ and _____ and _____, the testator and the witnesses, whose names are signed to the attached or foregoing instrument in those capacities, personally appearing before the undersigned authority and being first duly sworn, declare to the undersigned authority under penalty of perjury that: 1) the testator declared, signed, and executed the instrument as a codicil to his or her last will; 2) he or she signed it willingly, or directed another to sign for him or her; 3) he or she executed it as his or her free and voluntary act for the purposes therein expressed; and 4) each of the witnesses, at the request of the testator, in his or her hearing and presence and in the presence of each other, signed the will as witnesses, and that to the best of his or her knowledge the testator was at that time of full legal age, of sound mind, and under no constraint or undue influence.

_____ (Testator)

_____ (Witness)

_____ (Witness)

Subscribed, sworn, and acknowledged before me _____ a notary public, and by _____, the testator, and by _____ and _____, witnesses, this _____ day of _____, 20_____.

_____
Notary public

This page intentionally blank.

Self-Proved Codicil Affidavit
(attach to Codicil)

STATE OF _____

COUNTY OF _____

I, the undersigned, an officer authorized to administer oaths, certify that _____ _____, the testator and _____ and _____, the witnesses, whose names are signed to the attached or foregoing instrument and whose signatures appear below, having appeared before me and having first been duly sworn, each then declared to me that: 1) the attached or foregoing instrument is a codicil to the last will of the testator; 2) the testator willingly and voluntarily declared, signed, and executed the will in the presence of the witnesses; 3) the witnesses signed the will upon the request of the testator, in the presence and hearing of the testator and in the presence of each other; 4) to the best knowledge of each witness, the testator was, at the time of signing, of the age of majority (or otherwise legally competent to make a will), of sound mind and memory, and under no constraint or undue influence; and 5) each witness was and is competent and of proper age to witness a codicil to a will.

_____ (Testator)

_____ (Witness)

_____ (Witness)

Subscribed and sworn to before me by _____, the testator, who is personally known to me or who has produced _____ as identification, and by _____ a witness who is personally known to me or who has produced _____ as identification, and by _____, a witness, who is personally known to me or who has produced _____ as identification, this _____ day of _____, 20____.

_____
Notary or other officer

This page intentionally blank.

Self-Proved Codicil Affidavit
(attach to Codicil)

STATE OF TEXAS

COUNTY OF _____

Before me, the undersigned authority, on this day personally appeared _____
_____, _____, and
_____, known to me to be the testator and the
witnesses, respectively, whose names are subscribed to the annexed or foregoing
instrument in their respective capacities, and, all of said persons being by me duly
sworn, the said _____ testator, declared to me
and to the said witnesses in my presence that said instrument is his or her codicil, and
that he or she had willingly made and executed it as his or her free act and deed, and
the said witnesses, each on his or her oath stated to me in the presence and hearing of
the said testator, that the said testator had declared to them that said instrument is his
or her codicil, and that he or she executed same as such and wanted each of them to
sign it as a witness; and upon their oaths each witness stated further that they did sign
the same as witnesses in the presence of the said testator and at his or her request;
that he or she was at the time eighteen years of age or over (or being under such age,
was or had been lawfully married, or was then a member of the armed forces of the
United States or an auxiliary thereof or of the Maritime Service) and was of sound mind;
and that each of said witnesses was then at least fourteen years of age.

_____ (Testator)

_____ (Witness)

_____ (Witness)

Subscribed and sworn to before me by _____, the testator, and
by _____, and _____,
the witnesses, this _____ day of _____, 20____.

Signed: _____

_____
Official Capacity of Officer

This page intentionally blank.

Living Will

I, _____, _____ (d/o/b) being of sound mind willfully and voluntarily make known my desires regarding my medical care and treatment under the circumstances as indicated below:

_____   1. If I should have an incurable or irreversible condition that will cause my death within a relatively short time, and if I am unable to make decisions regarding my medical treatment, I direct my attending physician to withhold or withdraw procedures that merely prolong the dying process and are not necessary to my comfort or to alleviate pain. This authorization includes, but is not limited to, the withholding or the withdrawal of the following types of medical treatment (subject to any special instructions in paragraph 5 below):

_____   a. Artificial feeding and hydration.
_____   b. Cardiopulmonary resuscitation (this includes, but is not limited to, the use of drugs, electric shock, and artificial breathing).
_____   c. Kidney dialysis.
_____   d. Surgery or other invasive procedures.
_____   e. Drugs and antibiotics.
_____   f. Transfusions of blood or blood products.
_____   g. Other: _____
             _____

_____   2. If I should be in an irreversible coma or persistent vegetative state that my attending physician reasonably believes to be irreversible or incurable, I direct my attending physician to withhold or withdraw medical procedures and treatment other than such medical procedures and treatment necessary to my comfort or to alleviate pain. This authorization includes, but is not limited to, the withholding or withdrawal of the following types of medical treatment (subject to any special instructions in paragraph 5 below):

_____   a. Artificial feeding and hydration.
_____   b. Cardiopulmonary resuscitation (this includes, but is not limited to, the use of drugs, electric shock, and artificial breathing).
_____   c. Kidney dialysis.
_____   d. Surgery or other invasive procedures.
_____   e. Drugs and antibiotics.
_____   f. Transfusions of blood or blood products.
_____   g. Other: _____
             _____

_____   3.   If I have a medical condition where I am unable to communicate my desires as to treatment and my physician determines that the burdens of treatment outweigh the expected benefits, I direct my attending physician to withhold or withdraw medical procedures and treatment other than such medical procedures and treatment necessary to my comfort or to alleviate pain. This authorization includes, but is not limited to, the withholding or withdrawal of the following types of medical treatment (subject to any special instructions in paragraph 5 below):

_____   a. Artificial feeding and hydration.

_____   b. Cardiopulmonary resuscitation (this includes, but is not limited to, the use of drugs, electric shock, and artificial breathing).

_____   c. Kidney dialysis.

_____   d. Surgery or other invasive procedures.

_____   e. Drugs and antibiotics.

_____   f. Transfusions of blood or blood products.

_____   g. Other: _____
_____

_____   4. I want my life prolonged to the greatest extent possible (subject to any special instructions in paragraph 5 below).

_____   5. Special instructions (if any) _____
_____
_____
_____

Signed this _____ day of _____, 200____.

_____
Signature

Address: _____
_____

The declarant is personally known to me and voluntarily signed this document in my presence.

Witness: _____   Witness _____
Name: _____   Name: _____
Address: _____   Address: _____

State of   _____)
County of   _____)

On this _____ day of _____, 200_____, before me, personally appeared _____, principal, and _____ and _____, witnesses, who are personally known to me or who provided _____ as identification, and signed the foregoing instrument in my presence.

_____
Notary Public

General Power of Attorney

_____ (the Grantor)
hereby grants to _____
(the Agent) a general power of attorney. As the Grantor's attorney in fact, the Agent shall have full power and authority to undertake any and all acts, which may be lawfully undertaken on behalf of the grantor, including but not limited to: the right to buy, sell, lease, mortgage, assign, rent, or otherwise dispose of any real or personal property belonging to the Grantor; to execute, accept, undertake, and perform contracts in the name of the Grantor; to deposit, endorse, or withdraw funds to or from any bank depository of the Grantor; to initiate, defend, or settle legal actions on behalf of the Grantor; and to retain any accountant, attorney or other advisor deemed by the Agent to be necessary to protect the interests of the Grantor in relation to such powers.

By accepting this grant, the Agent agrees to act in a fiduciary capacity consistent with the reasonable best interests of the Grantor. This power of attorney may be revoked by the Grantor at any time; however, any person dealing with the Agent as attorney in fact may rely on this appointment until receipt of actual notice of termination.

IN WITNESS WHEREOF, the undersigned grantor has executed this power of attorney under seal as of the date stated above.

_____(Seal)
Grantor

STATE OF
COUNTY OF

I certify that _____, who
☐ is personally known to me to be the person whose name is subscribed to the foregoing instrument ☐ produced _____ as identification, personally appeared before me on _____, 20_____, and acknowledged the execution of the foregoing instrument.

_____
Notary Public, State of
Notary's commission expires:

I hereby accept the foregoing appointment as attorney in fact on _____, 20_____.

_____
Attorney in Fact

This page intentionally blank.

Specific Power of Attorney

_____ (the Grantor) hereby grants to _____ (the Agent) a limited power of attorney. As the Grantor's attorney in fact, the Agent shall have full power and authority to undertake and perform the following on behalf of the Grantor:

By accepting this grant, the Agent agrees to act in a fiduciary capacity consistent with the reasonable best interests of the Grantor. This power of attorney may be revoked by the Grantor at any time; however, any person dealing with the Agent as attorney in fact may rely on this appointment until receipt of actual notice of termination.

IN WITNESS WHEREOF, the undersigned grantor has executed this power of attorney under seal as of the date stated above.

_____(Seal)
Grantor

STATE OF
COUNTY OF

I certify that _____, who □ is personally known to me to be the person whose name is subscribed to the foregoing instrument □ produced _____ as identification, personally appeared before me on _____, 20_____, and acknowledged the execution of the foregoing instrument.

_____
Notary Public, State of
Notary's commission expires:

I hereby accept the foregoing appointment as attorney in fact on _____, 20_____.

_____
Attorney in Fact

This page intentionally blank.

Revocation of Power of Attorney

I, _____ (the Grantor) granted
a Power of Attorney to _____
(the Agent) dated _____, do hereby revoke said Power of Attorney
as of _____, 20___.

STATE OF
COUNTY OF

I certify that _____, who
☐ is personally known to me to be the person whose name is subscribed to the
foregoing instrument ☐ produced _____ as
identification, personally appeared before me on _____, 20_____,
and acknowledged the execution of the foregoing instrument.

_____
Notary Public, State of
Notary's commission expires:

This page intentionally blank.

Health Care Power of Attorney

I, _____,
as principal, designate _____
as my agent for all matters relating to my health care, including, without limitation, full power to give or refuse consent to all medical, surgical, hospital, and related health care. This power of attorney is effective on my inability to make or communicate health care decisions. All of my agent's actions under this power during any period when I am unable to make or communicate health care decisions or when there is uncertainty whether I am dead or alive have the same effect on my heirs, devisees, and personal representatives as if I were alive, competent, and acting for myself.

If my agent is unwilling or unable to serve or continue to serve, I hereby appoint _____ as my agent.

☐ I have   ☐ I have not completed and attached a living will for purposes of providing specific direction to my agent in situations that may occur during any period when I am unable to make or communicate health care decisions or after my death. My agent is directed to implement those choices I have initialed in the living will.

This health care directive continues in effect for all who may rely on it except those to whom I have given notice of its revocation.

_____   _____
Witness   Signature of Principal

_____   _____
Address   Date

_____   _____
Witness   Time

_____   _____
Address   Address of Agent

                                       _____
                                       Telephone of Agent

This page intentionally blank.

Uniform Organ Donor Card

UNIFORM DONOR CARD

The undersigned hereby makes this anatomical gift, if medically acceptable, to take effect on death. The words and marks below indicate my desires:

I give:

(a) _____ any needed organs or parts;

(b) _____ only the following organs or parts

_____

for the purpose of transplantation, therapy, medical research, or education;

(c) _____ my body for anatomical study if needed.

Limitations or special wishes, if any:

_____

_____

Signed by the donor and the following witnesses in the presence of each other:

_____   _____
Signature of Donor   Date of birth

_____   _____
Date signed   City & State

_____   _____
Witness   Witness

_____   _____
Address   Address

UNIFORM DONOR CARD

The undersigned hereby makes this anatomical gift, if medically acceptable, to take effect on death. The words and marks below indicate my desires:

I give:

(a) _____ any needed organs or parts;

(b) _____ only the following organs or parts

_____

for the purpose of transplantation, therapy, medical research, or education;

(c) _____ my body for anatomical study if needed.

Limitations or special wishes, if any:

_____

_____

Signed by the donor and the following witnesses in the presence of each other:

_____   _____
Signature of Donor   Date of birth

_____   _____
Date signed   City & State

_____   _____
Witness   Witness

_____   _____
Address   Address

UNIFORM DONOR CARD

The undersigned hereby makes this anatomical gift, if medically acceptable, to take effect on death. The words and marks below indicate my desires:

I give:

(a) _____ any needed organs or parts;

(b) _____ only the following organs or parts

_____

for the purpose of transplantation, therapy, medical research, or education;

(c) _____ my body for anatomical study if needed.

Limitations or special wishes, if any:

_____

_____

Signed by the donor and the following witnesses in the presence of each other:

_____   _____
Signature of Donor   Date of birth

_____   _____
Date signed   City & State

_____   _____
Witness   Witness

_____   _____
Address   Address

UNIFORM DONOR CARD

The undersigned hereby makes this anatomical gift, if medically acceptable, to take effect on death. The words and marks below indicate my desires:

I give:

(a) _____ any needed organs or parts;

(b) _____ only the following organs or parts

_____

for the purpose of transplantation, therapy, medical research, or education;

(c) _____ my body for anatomical study if needed.

Limitations or special wishes, if any:

_____

_____

Signed by the donor and the following witnesses in the presence of each other:

_____   _____
Signature of Donor   Date of birth

_____   _____
Date signed   City & State

_____   _____
Witness   Witness

_____   _____
Address   Address

This page intentionally blank.

Living Trust

THE

_____

REVOCABLE LIVING TRUST

I, _____, of _____
_____, hereby make and declare this Living Trust, as Grantor and Trustee, on _____, 20____.

This Trust shall be known as the _____
Revocable Living Trust. I, _____, will be trustee of this trust. Upon my death or if I am unable to manage this trust and my financial affairs, I appoint _____, my _____, of _____
_____ as successor trustee, to serve without bond. In addition to any powers, authority, and discretion granted by law, I grant such Trustee and Successor Trustee any and all powers to perform any acts, in his or her sole discretion and without court approval, for the management and distribution of this trust.

TRANSFER OF PROPERTY. I hereby transfer to this trust the property listed on the attached Schedule of Assets which is made a part of this trust. I shall have the right at any time to add property to the trust or delete property from the trust.

DISPOSITION OF INCOME AND PRINCIPAL. During my lifetime, the Trustee shall pay so much or all of the net income and principal of the trust as I from time to time may request to me. Upon my death, the successor trustee shall pay all claims, expenses and taxes and shall distribute the trust estate to the following beneficiary or beneficiaries who shall survive me:

_____
_____
_____
_____
_____

The share of a beneficiary who is under _____ years of age shall not be paid to such beneficiary but shall be held in trust by the Trustee. The Trustee shall pay so much or all of the net income and principal of such trust to the beneficiary as he thinks necessary for his or her support, welfare, and education. The Trustee shall pay the beneficiary the remaining principal, if any, when he or she attains the age of _____ years.

In case a beneficiary for whom a share is held in trust dies before receiving the remaining principal, it shall be paid to his or her living child or children, or if none, to my then living descendants.

This trust shall terminate twenty-one (21) years after the death of the last beneficiary named in the trust.

REVOCATION AND AMENDMENT. I may, by signed instrument delivered to the Trustee, revoke or amend this Trust Agreement in whole or in part.

GOVERNING LAW. This Trust will be governed under the laws of the State of _____.

In Witness Whereof, I as Grantor and Trustee, have executed this Agreement on the date above written.

_____   _____
Witness   Grantor

_____   _____
Witness   Trustee

STATE OF _____   )
COUNTY OF _____   )

The foregoing instrument was acknowledged before me this _____ day of _____, 20___, by _____, as Grantor and Trustee, who is personally known to me or who has produced _____ as identification.

_____
Notary Public
My Commission Expires:

Living Trust—Schedule of Assets

This Schedule of Assets of Living Trust is attached and made part of the _____
_____ Revocable Living Trust, dated _____,
20____.

The following assets are made part of this Living Trust:

This page intentionally blank.

Declaration of Joint Property

The undersigned, in consideration of the mutual agreement herein contained, agree that all property owned by them and located in their place of residence shall be owned in joint tenancy with full rights of survivorship, except the following items, which shall remain separate property for all purposes:

In addition to the property located at the residence, the following property shall also be owned in joint tenancy with full rights of survivorship:

In witness whereof, the parties affix their signatures and seals this _____ day of _____, 20_____.

_____ (seal)

_____ (seal)

This page intentionally blank.

Declaration of Separate Property

The undersigned, in consideration of the mutual agreement herein contained, agree that all property owned by them and located in their place of residence shall be owned as separate property of the person by whom it was purchased, except the following items, which are owned as joint property with full rights of survivorship.

In addition to the property located at the residence, the following property shall also be owned as separate property:

In witness whereof, the parties affix their signatures and seals this _____ day of _____, 20_____.

_____ (seal)

_____ (seal)

This page intentionally blank.

Living Trust—Amendment

AMENDMENT TO THE

_____

REVOCABLE LIVING TRUST

This Amendment to the _____ Revocable Living
Trust, dated _____, 20 ____, is made by _____,
Grantor, on _____, 20____.

The Grantor hereby amends the Trust as follows:

State of _____
County of _____

On _____, 20_____, before me personally appeared
_____, who is personally known to me or who
provided _____ as identification,
and signed the above document in my presence.

_____
Notary Public
My Commission expires:

This page intentionally blank.

Living Trust—Termination

I, _____, of _____
_____, hereby revoke the
_____ Living Trust, dated _____,
20_____.

Dated: _____, 20_____

_____
Grantor

State of _____
County of _____

On _____, 20_____, before me personally appeared
_____, who is personally known to me or who
provided _____ as identification,
and signed the above document in my presence.

_____
Notary Public
My Commission expires:

This page intentionally blank.

Notice of Death to Social Security Administration

To: Social Security Administration

_____

_____

This letter is to inform you that _____
whose Social Security number is _____-_____-_____, and resided at
_____, died on _____,
20_____.

Any payments made after death are being returned with this letter or will be returned as received. Please stop all future payments.

Sincerely,

_____

_____

_____

Index

SPHINX® PUBLISHING ORDER FORM

BILL TO:			SHIP TO:		

Phone #		Terms		F.O.B.	Chicago, IL	Ship Date

Charge my: ☐ VISA ☐ MasterCard ☐ American Express

☐ **Money Order or Personal Check**

Credit Card Number

Expiration Date

Qty	ISBN	Title	Retail	Ext.
		SPHINX PUBLISHING NATIONAL TITLES		
	1-57248-363-6	101 Complaint Letters That Get Results	$18.95	
	1-57248-361-X	The 529 College Savings Plan (2E)	$18.95	
	1-57248-483-7	The 529 College Savings Plan Made Simple	$7.95	
	1-57248-460-8	The Alternative Minimum Tax	$14.95	
	1-57248-349-0	The Antique and Art Collector's Legal Guide	$24.95	
	1-57248-347-4	Attorney Responsibilities & Client Rights	$19.95	
	1-57248-482-9	The Childcare Answer Book	$12.95	
	1-57248-382-2	Child Support	$18.95	
	1-57248-487-X	Cómo Comprar su Primera Casa	$8.95	
	1-57248-488-8	Cómo Conseguir Trabajo en los Estados Unidos	$8.95	
	1-57248-148-X	Cómo Hacer su Propio Testamento	$16.95	
	1-57248-532-9	Cómo Iniciar su Propio Negocio	$8.95	
	1-57248-462-4	Cómo Negociar su Crédito	$8.95	
	1-57248-463-2	Cómo Organizar un Presupuesto	$8.95	
	1-57248-147-1	Cómo Solicitar su Propio Divorcio	$24.95	
	1-57248-507-8	The Complete Book of Corporate Forms (2E)	$29.95	
	1-57248-383-0	The Complete Book of Insurance	$18.95	
	1-57248499-3	The Complete Book of Personal Legal Forms	$24.95	
	1-57248-528-0	The Complete Book of Real Estate Contracts	$18.95	
	1-57248-500-0	The Complete Credit Repair Kit	$19.95	
	1-57248-458-6	The Complete Hiring and Firing Handbook	$18.95	
	1-57248-484-5	The Complete Home-Based Business Kit	$16.95	
	1-57248-353-9	The Complete Kit to Selling Your Own Home	$18.95	
	1-57248-229-X	The Complete Legal Guide to Senior Care	$21.95	
	1-57248-498-5	The Complete Limited Liability Company Kit	$24.95	
	1-57248-391-1	The Complete Partnership Book	$24.95	
	1-57248-201-X	The Complete Patent Book	$26.95	
	1-57248-514-0	The Complete Patent Kit	$39.95	
	1-57248-480-2	The Mortgage Answer Book	$14.95	
	1-57248-369-5	Credit Smart	$18.95	
	1-57248-163-3	Crime Victim's Guide to Justice (2E)	$21.95	
	1-57248-481-0	The Easy Will and Living Will Kit	$16.95	
	1-57248-251-6	The Entrepreneur's Internet Handbook	$21.95	
	1-57248-235-4	The Entrepreneur's Legal Guide	$26.95	
	1-57248-160-9	Essential Guide to Real Estate Leases	$18.95	
	1-57248-375-X	Fathers' Rights	$19.95	
	1-57248-517-5	File Your Own Divorce (6E)	$24.95	
	1-57248-553-1	Financing Your Small Business	$16.95	
	1-57248-459-4	Fired, Laid Off or Forced Out	$14.95	
	1-57248-502-7	The Frequent Traveler's Guide	$14.95	
	1-57248-331-8	Gay & Lesbian Rights	$26.95	
	1-57248-526-4	Grandparents' Rights (4E)	$24.95	
	1-57248-475-6	Guía de Inmigración a Estados Unidos (4E)	$24.95	
	1-57248-187-0	Guía de Justicia para Víctimas del Crimen	$21.95	
	1-57248-253-2	Guía Esencial para los Contratos de Arrendamiento de Bienes Raices	$22.95	
	1-57248-334-2	Homeowner's Rights	$19.95	
	1-57248-164-1	How to Buy a Condominium or Townhome (2E)	$19.95	
	1-57248-197-7	How to Buy Your First Home (2E)	$14.95	
	1-57248-384-9	How to Buy a Franchise	$19.95	
	1-57248-472-1	How to File Your Own Bankruptcy (6E)	$21.95	
	1-57248-390-3	How to Form a Nonprofit Corporation (3E)	$24.95	
	1-57248-345-8	How to Form Your Own Corporation (4E)	$26.95	

Qty	ISBN	Title	Retail	Ext.
	1-57248-520-5	How to Make Money on Foreclosures	$16.95	
	1-57248-479-9	How to Parent with Your Ex	$12.95	
	1-57248-379-2	How to Register Your Own Copyright (5E)	$24.95	
	1-57248-394-6	How to Write Your Own Living Will (4E)	$18.95	
	1-57248-156-0	How to Write Your Own Premarital Agreement (3E)	$24.95	
	1-57248-504-3	HR for Small Business	$14.95	
	1-57248-230-3	Incorporate in Delaware from Any State	$26.95	
	1-57248-158-7	Incorporate in Nevada from Any State	$24.95	
	1-57248-531-0	The Infertility Answer Book	$16.95	
	1-57248-474-8	Inmigración a los EE.UU. Paso a Paso (2E)	$24.95	
	1-57248-400-4	Inmigración y Ciudadanía en los EE.UU. Preguntas y Respuestas	$16.95	
	1-57248-453-5	Law 101	$16.95	
	1-57248-374-1	Law School 101	$16.95	
	1-57248-377-6	The Law (In Plain English)® for Small Business	$19.95	
	1-57248-476-4	The Law (In Plain English)® for Writers	$14.95	
	1-57248-509-4	Legal Research Made Easy (4E)	$24.95	
	1-57248-449-7	The Living Trust Kit	$21.95	
	1-57248-165-X	Living Trusts and Other Ways to Avoid Probate (3E)	$24.95	
	1-57248-511-6	Make Your Own Simple Will (4E)	$26.95	
	1-57248-486-1	Making Music Your Business	$18.95	
	1-57248-186-2	Manual de Beneficios para el Seguro Social	$18.95	
	1-57248-220-6	Mastering the MBE	$16.95	
	1-57248-455-1	Minding Her Own Business, 4E	$14.95	
	1-57248-480-2	The Mortgage Answer Book	$14.95	
	1-57248-167-6	Most Val. Business Legal Forms You'll Ever Need (3E)	$21.95	
	1-57248-388-1	The Power of Attorney Handbook (5E)	$22.95	
	1-57248-332-6	Profit from Intellectual Property	$28.95	
	1-57248-329-6	Protect Your Patent	$24.95	
	1-57248-376-8	Nursing Homes and Assisted Living Facilities	$19.95	
	1-57248-385-7	Quick Cash	$14.95	
	1-57248-350-4	El Seguro Social Preguntas y Respuestas	$16.95	
	1-57248-529-9	Sell Your Home Without a Broker	$14.95	
	1-57248386-5	Seniors' Rights	$19.95	
	1-57248-527-2	Sexual Harassment in the Workplace	$18.95	
	1-57248-217-6	Sexual Harassment: Your Guide to Legal Action	$18.95	
	1-57248-378-4	Sisters-in-Law	$16.95	
	1-57248-219-2	The Small Business Owner's Guide to Bankruptcy	$21.95	
	1-57248-395-4	The Social Security Benefits Handbook (4E)	$18.95	
	1-57248-216-8	Social Security Q&A	$12.95	
	1-57248-521-3	Start Your Own Law Practice	$16.95	
	1-57248-328-8	Starting Out or Starting Over	$14.95	
	1-57248-525-6	Teen Rights (and Responsibilities) (2E)	$14.95	
	1-57248-457-8	Tax Power for the Self-Employed	$17.95	
	1-57248-366-0	Tax Smarts for Small Business	$21.95	
	1-57248-530-2	Unmarried Parents' Rights (3E)	$16.95	
	1-57248-362-8	U.S. Immigration and Citizenship Q&A	$18.95	
	1-57248-387-3	U.S. Immigration Step by Step (2E)	$24.95	
	1-57248-392-X	U.S.A. Immigration Guide (5E)	$26.95	
	1-57248-178-0	¡Visas! ¡Visas! ¡Visas!	$9.95	
	1-57248-177-2	The Weekend Landlord	$16.95	
	1-57248-451-9	What to Do—Before "I DO"	$14.95	

(Form Continued on Following Page) Subtotal _____

To order, call Sourcebooks at 1-800-432-7444 or FAX (630) 961-2168 (Bookstores, libraries, wholesalers—please call for discount)

Prices are subject to change without notice.

Find more legal information at: **www.SphinxLegal.com**

SPHINX® PUBLISHING ORDER FORM

Qty	ISBN	Title	Retail	Ext.
____	1-57248-225-7	Win Your Unemployment Compensation Claim (2E)	$21.95	____
____	1-57248-330-X	The Wills, Estate Planning and Trusts Legal Kit	$26.95	____
____	1-57248-473-X	Winning Your Personal Injury Claim (3E)	$24.95	____
____	1-57248-333-4	Working with Your Homeowners Association	$19.95	____
____	1-57248-380-6	Your Right to Child Custody, Visitation and Support (3E)	$24.95	____
____	1-57248-505-1	Your Rights at Work	$14.95	____

CALIFORNIA TITLES

Qty	ISBN	Title	Retail	Ext.
____	1-57248-489-6	How to File for Divorce in CA (5E)	$26.95	____
____	1-57248-464-0	How to Settle and Probate an Estate in CA (2E)	$28.95	____
____	1-57248-336-9	How to Start a Business in CA (2E)	$21.95	____
____	1-57248-194-3	How to Win in Small Claims Court in CA (2E)	$18.95	____
____	1-57248-246-X	Make Your Own CA Will	$18.95	____
____	1-57248-397-0	Landlords' Legal Guide in CA (2E)	$24.95	____
____	1-57248-515-9	Tenants' Rights in CA (2E)	$24.95	____

FLORIDA TITLES

Qty	ISBN	Title	Retail	Ext.
____	1-57248-396-2	How to File for Divorce in FL (8E)	$28.95	____
____	1-57248-356-3	How to Form a Corporation in FL (6E)	$24.95	____
____	1-57248-490-X	How to Form a Limited Liability Co. in FL (4E)	$24.95	____
____	1-57071-401-0	How to Form a Partnership in FL	$22.95	____
____	1-57248-456-X	How to Make a FL Will (7E)	$16.95	____
____	1-57248-354-7	How to Probate and Settle an Estate in FL (5E)	$26.95	____
____	1-57248-339-3	How to Start a Business in FL (7E)	$21.95	____
____	1-57248-204-4	How to Win in Small Claims Court in FL (7E)	$18.95	____
____	1-57248-381-4	Land Trusts in Florida (7E)	$29.95	____
____	1-57248-491-8	Landlords' Rights and Duties in FL (10E)	$22.95	____

GEORGIA TITLES

Qty	ISBN	Title	Retail	Ext.
____	1-57248-340-7	How to File for Divorce in GA (5E)	$21.95	____
____	1-57248-493-4	How to Start a Business in GA (4E)	$21.95	____

ILLINOIS TITLES

Qty	ISBN	Title	Retail	Ext.
____	1-57248-244-3	Child Custody, Visitation, and Support in IL	$24.95	____
____	1-57248-206-0	How to File for Divorce in IL (3E)	$24.95	____
____	1-57248-170-6	How to Make an IL Will (3E)	$16.95	____
____	1-57248-265-9	How to Start a Business in IL (4E)	$21.95	____
____	1-57248-252-4	Landlords' Legal Guide in IL	$24.95	____

MARYLAND, VIRGINIA AND THE DISTRICT OF COLUMBIA

Qty	ISBN	Title	Retail	Ext.
____	1-57248-240-0	How to File for Divorce in MD, VA, and DC	$28.95	____
____	1-57248-359-8	How to Start a Business in MD, VA, or DC	$21.95	____

MASSACHUSETTS TITLES

Qty	ISBN	Title	Retail	Ext.
____	1-57248-115-3	How to Form a Corporation in MA	$24.95	____
____	1-57248-466-7	How to Start a Business in MA (4E)	$21.95	____
____	1-57248-398-9	Landlords' Legal Guide in MA (2E)	$24.95	____

MICHIGAN TITLES

Qty	ISBN	Title	Retail	Ext.
____	1-57248-467-5	How to File for Divorce in MI (4E)	$24.95	____
____	1-57248-182-X	How to Make a MI Will (3E)	$16.95	____
____	1-57248-468-3	How to Start a Business in MI (4E)	$18.95	____

MINNESOTA TITLES

Qty	ISBN	Title	Retail	Ext.
____	1-57248-142-0	How to File for Divorce in MN	$21.95	____
____	1-57248-179-X	How to Form a Corporation in MN	$24.95	____
____	1-57248-178-1	How to Make a MN Will (2E)	$16.95	____

NEW JERSEY TITLES

Qty	ISBN	Title	Retail	Ext.
____	1-57248-512-4	File for Divorce in NJ (2E)	$24.95	____
____	1-57248-448-9	How to Start a Business in NJ	$21.95	____

NEW YORK TITLES

Qty	ISBN	Title	Retail	Ext.
____	1-57248-193-5	Child Custody, Visitation and Support in NY	$26.95	____
____	1-57248-351-2	File for Divorce in NY	$26.95	____
____	1-57248-249-4	How to Form a Corporation in NY (2E)	$24.95	____
____	1-57248-401-2	How to Make a NY Will (3E)	$16.95	____
____	1-57248-469-1	How to Start a Business in NY (3E)	$21.95	____
____	1-57248-198-6	How to Win in Small Claims Court in NY (2E)	$18.95	____
____	1-57248-122-6	Tenants' Rights in NY	$21.95	____

NORTH CAROLINA AND SOUTH CAROLINA TITLES

Qty	ISBN	Title	Retail	Ext.
____	1-57248-508-6	How to File for Divorce in NC (4E)	$26.95	____
____	1-57248-371-7	How to Start a Business in NC or SC	$24.95	____
____	1-57248-091-2	Landlords' Rights & Duties in NC	$21.95	____

OHIO TITLES

Qty	ISBN	Title	Retail	Ext.
____	1-57248-503-5	How to File for Divorce in OH (3E)	$24.95	____
____	1-57248-174-9	How to Form a Corporation in OH	$24.95	____
____	1-57248-173-0	How to Make an OH Will	$16.95	____

PENNSYLVANIA TITLES

Qty	ISBN	Title	Retail	Ext.
____	1-57248-242-7	Child Custody, Visitation and Support in PA	$26.95	____
____	1-57248-495-0	How to File for Divorce in PA (4E)	$24.95	____
____	1-57248-358-X	How to Form a Corporation in PA	$24.95	____
____	1-57248-094-7	How to Make a PA Will (2E)	$16.95	____
____	1-57248-357-1	How to Start a Business in PA (3E)	$21.95	____
____	1-57248-245-1	Landlords' Legal Guide in PA	$24.95	____

TEXAS TITLES

Qty	ISBN	Title	Retail	Ext.
____	1-57248-171-4	Child Custody, Visitation, and Support in TX	$22.95	____
____	1-57248-399-7	How to File for Divorce in TX (4E)	$24.95	____
____	1-57248-470-5	How to Form a Corporation in TX (3E)	$24.95	____
____	1-57248-496-9	How to Probate and Settle an Estate in TX (4E)	$26.95	____
____	1-57248-471-3	How to Start a Business in TX (4E)	$21.95	____
____	1-57248-111-0	How to Win in Small Claims Court in TX (2E)	$16.95	____
____	1-57248-355-5	Landlords' Legal Guide in TX	$24.95	____
____	1-57248-513-2	Write Your Own TX Will (4E)	$16.95	____

WASHINGTON TITLES

Qty	ISBN	Title	Retail	Ext.
____	1-57248-522-1	File for Divorce in WA	$24.95	____

SubTotal This page ____

SubTotal previous page ____

Shipping — $5.00 for 1st book, $1.00 each additional ____

Illinois residents add 6.75% sales tax ____

Connecticut residents add 6.00% sales tax ____

Total ____

To order, call Sourcebooks at 1-800-432-7444 or FAX (630) 961-2168 (Bookstores, libraries, wholesalers—please call for discount)

Prices are subject to change without notice.

Find more legal information at: **www.SphinxLegal.com**

How to Use the CD-ROM

Thank you for purchasing *Make Your Own Simple Will*. In this book, we have worked hard to compile exactly what you need to prepare and execute a will and other estate planning documents. To make this material even more useful, we have included every document in the book on the CD-ROM that is attached to the inside back cover of the book.

You can use these forms just as you would the forms in the book. Print them out, fill them in, and use them however you need. You can also fill in the forms directly on your computer. Just identify the form you need, open it, click on the space where the information should go, and input your information. Customize each form for your particular needs. Use them over and over again.

The CD-ROM is compatible with both PC and Mac operating systems. (While it should work with either operating system, we cannot guarantee that it will work with your particular system and we cannot provide technical assistance.) To use the forms on your computer, you will need to use Microsoft Word or another word processing program that can read Word files. The CD-ROM does not contain any such program.

Insert the CD-ROM into your computer. Double-click on the icon representing the disc on your desktop, or go through your hard drive to identify the drive that contains the disc and click on it.

Once opened, you will see the files contained on the CD-ROM listed as "Form #: [Form Title]." Open the file you need. You may print the form to fill it out manually at this point, or you can click on the appropriate line to fill it in using your computer.

Any time you see bracketed information [ ] on the form, you can click on it and delete the bracketed information from your final form. This information is only a reference guide to assist you in filling in the forms and should be removed from your final version. Once all your information is filled in, you can print your filled-in form.

• • • • •

Purchasers of this book are granted a license to use the forms contained in it for their own personal use. By purchasing this book, you have also purchased a limited license to use all forms on the accompanying CD-ROM. The license limits you to personal use only and all other copyright laws must be adhered to. No claim of copyright is made in any government form reproduced in the book or on the CD-ROM. You are free to modify the forms and tailor them to your specific situation.

The author and publisher have attempted to provide the most current and up-to-date information available. However, the courts, Congress, and your state's legislatures review, modify, and change laws on an ongoing basis, as well as create new laws from time to time. Due to the very nature of the information and the continual changes in our legal system, to be sure that you have the current and best information for your situation, you should consult a local attorney or research the current laws yourself.

This publication is designed to provide accurate and authoritative information in regard to the subject matter covered. It is sold with the understanding that the publisher is not engaged in rendering legal, accounting, or other professional service. If legal advice or other expert assistance is required, the services of a competent professional person should be sought.

> —*From a Declaration of Principles Jointly Adopted by a Committee of the American Bar Association and a Committee of Publishers and Associations*

This product is not a substitute for legal advice.

> —*Disclaimer required by Texas statutes*